No Love, *No* Charity
The Success of the 19ᵗʰ Child

by

Paul Lamar Hunter

© 2012

Life To Legacy, LLC

No Love, No Charity:
The Success of the 19th Child

Printed in the United States

ISBN-10: 0984797343
ISBN-13: 978-0-9847973-4-9

Interior and Cover design by:
Latoya Bady,
TBady Graphic Designs
Chicago, Illinois
Tbady@live.com

Edited by: Val Hennen
valhennen@yahoo.com

Published by: Life To Legacy, LLC
20650 Cicero Ave, #1239
Matteson, IL 60443
(877) 267-7477
www.Life2Legacy.com

Presented To:

To contact Paul Hunter
send email to:
Paul@NoLoveNoCharity.com
or
visit Paul's website
www.NoLoveNoCharity.com

Contents

WHAT PEOPLE ARE SAYING

This book is a dark revelation about how traumatic growing up can be. Paul's story reiterates the fact that those of us who have loving parents are truly blessed. As I read this book, I can relate to Paul's pain as my mother also placed herself first—ahead of myself and my siblings. I came to this realization as my wife demonstrated unselfish, self-sacrificing love towards our two children. I also recall that growing up as a child, one of the most painful things for me to witness was the wonderful relationship that my friends had with their mothers. Though I was happy for my friends, it still reminded me of what I was missing—a relationship with my mother. That was something I could have only wished for. How can one give something that they have never had, especially when that something is love? That's why I'm so grateful for my wife and children. But Paul's story will encourage anyone that he or she can make it despite all the odds. Certainly, it can be done. It should be done. It must be done.

Kevin Weslaski

Image Management, LLC

Racine, Wisconsin

A truly compelling and very interesting book. It holds your attention from beginning to end. A must read!

Attorney Thomas W. Durkin

Racine, Wisconsin

The phrase "reality is stranger than fiction" certainly applies to this poignant story. However, the darkness does not overtake the light. Truly, an overcomer's story. In the end, Paul Hunter prevails.

The Publisher

Acknowledgements

I would like to personally thank the following individuals and entities listed below for playing an integral part in helping me become the man I am today. Whether it was through personal contact or through inspiration at a distance, you have helped me in more ways than you will ever know. I thank God for each of you and continue to ask His blessing upon you all.

Individuals

NBA All-Star Caron Butler, Tom Joyner, Tavis Smiley, Portia Young, Dr. Dennis J. Woods, Roland Martin, Pastor Jeff & Tami Butler, Carole Meekins, Pastor Frank & Yolanda James, Joel Osteen, Monica Jones, Pastor Randy Cameron, Jacque Reid, Dr. Jim Ward, Valerie Hennen, Alex Scales, Amy Adair, Romeo Bouie, Nina Hemphill, Gerald D. Wright, Scott Terry, Earl Stokes, Lauri Jones, Jeff Collen, Armstrong Williams, Kim Buchanan, Carole Aeschelmann, Stephanie Jones, L. A. Justice, Samantha Schiro, Jameeka Bouie, Karen Zuker, Nancy Jeffrey, Paul Northam, Lynne Zygowski, Marshall Whitlock, Gloria Lezala, Tracy Jallah, Noel Niemann, Leroy Kolacinski, Billy Boyd, Alonzo Payne, Jasmine Lohr, Christopher Bogan, Patrick McHugh, Michael Scholz, Breann McCarty, Janet Days, Derrick Brown, Donnie Gardner, Professor Steven Smith, Larry McGee, Emily Moser, Jordan Payne, Vicki Bott, Kimberly Hope Bright, Larry Kirkwood, Steven E. Heitman, Cathy Orosz, Molly Fay, Tiffany Ogle, Nina Thompson, Monica Bayer Heaton, Kevin Weslaski, Hibo George, Professor Curt Weber, Kevin Brown, Melissa Barber, Richard Butler, Louis Rideaux, Manoj Babu, and James Winston.

ACKNOWLEDGEMENTS (CONT.)

Media

The Associated Press, Fox & Friends, The Tom Joyner Morning Show, the Tavis Smiley radio show, the Armstrong Williams radio show, Ebony Magazine, Today's Christian Magazine, Today's Black Woman, Gospel Today, AMPS magazine, Upscale Magazine, WISN 12 Milwaukee, WTMJ4 Milwaukee, WITI Fox 6 Milwaukee, National Examiner, Insider News, Racine, Wisconsin, Journal Times, Racine Wisconsin, Fayette Publishing, and The Morning Blend.

INTRODUCTION

Two thousand and six was a very interesting year. A lot of important milestones were accomplished in my personal life as well as in the lives of my immediate family, particularly that of my mother, Louise Hunter. When I look back at my life, I can say that up until a few years ago, I had always lived in the shadow of my larger-than-life mother, the matriarch of a large clan of over one hundred twenty children, grandchildren and great-grandchildren. Everyone else calls her "Mother Hunter." There is a lot of irony in her public name, particularly the "mother" part, seeing how none of her eighteen living children were ever allowed to call her that. We called her "E."

A year earlier, in 2005, my mother's long-anticipated book, *Love and Charity, the Life and Story of Louise Hunter, and the Love and Charity Homeless Shelter*, was finally released. That biography was a dramatic account of how my mother started her mission in Racine, Wisconsin, after being threatened with eviction while pregnant with my brother Larry, the fourteenth child, back in the early 1960s. With my parents having nowhere to go, a stranger showed up at the front door and gave them an eighteen-room house for the price of one dollar. It was truly a miracle. And that's what inspired my mother to start the Love and Charity mission.

Wow, everyone loved that story. So, when the book came out, there was a lot of hoopla already generated in the area of Racine, Wisconsin. In the past, many people had claimed they were going to write her book, and my mother always had a tendency to believe those who were simply blowing smoke; those were the ones she would usually swear by. But those who really loved and supported her somehow ended up on her bad side. Instead, she would always eventually turn against those who were standing in her corner.

A former resident of my mother's homeless shelter named Dennis Woods wrote my mother's book. She was thrilled, and our entire family was overjoyed. Dennis was a pleasant young minister from Chicago who had come to Love and Charity from another ministry named the Victory Center, also in Racine. The Victory Center was a ministry that specialized in recovery programs, and Dennis himself was a recovering addict.

After Dennis came to preach at Love and Charity one Sunday, my mother asked him to help her run the mission. Minister Woods, as my mother called him, was a mild-mannered, intelligent, and articulate young man. He was sincerely interested in helping my mother, but soon she and the mission were too much for him to handle, so he decided to leave. I felt sorry for him. My mother treated him like a dog, but like so many others that she mistreated, he didn't hold it against her and still found a way to come back and help Mother Hunter.

About a year after Dennis left, surprisingly he returned after he had gotten his first book published. Now Dennis' previous work had been published, and he was in a good position to write my mother's book. That was in 1995. Ten years later, it was 2005, and Dennis kept his word. He had finally completed the manuscript and made a book deal. With amazement, my mom was beaming, and my seventeen brothers and sisters were proud of her. If only for a moment in time, we were one big happy family.

To help promote my mom's book, I headed up the publicity campaign. Since my mother was well known throughout much of Wisconsin and her story was famous, it was easy to get Racine's Journal Times newspaper and Milwaukee's television news crews to cover her book release. I had a good time. It was a lot of fun. I called channels WTMJ 4, WISN 12, WITI Fox 6, and Fox and Friends to get news coverage, and each one of them agreed to cover the story. I worked extremely hard developing the publicity campaign that put my mother's story in front of the most respected news venues in the United States. If my mother would have had to pay an outside publicist to get her on the shows and in the magazines like I had, it wouldn't have happened because it would have cost thousands of dollars which she didn't have.

My mother, Dennis Woods, and I were on national programs like Tavis Smiley, Roland Martin, Tom Joyner, Chuck D, and Les Brown. Several other local radio and television shows aired programs dedicated to telling Louise Hunter's amazing story. Then there were the national magazines like *Christianity Today, Upscale, Sister 2 Sister* online, *Today's Black Woman, Gospel Today*, AMPS Magazine, and even a tabloid newspaper, the *National Examiner* which did stories on my mother's book. Whenever someone heard the Hunter story, they were excited and willing to have us on their show. There were book signings in Los Angeles, Chicago, Indianapolis, Springfield, Milwaukee, Racine, Kenosha, and other locations.

However, out of all of the media coverage that we received, the most exciting was when *Ebony Magazine* agreed to do our story. After weeks of telephone calls and negotiations, I convinced Ebony to do the story. Former *Ebony* writer Monica Jones was the journalist assigned to cover the story. Fourteen of my brothers and sisters came to the Mission to be included in the photograph. I called WISN 12 news and WITI Fox 6, who came down to cover the *Ebony* visit to Love and Charity.

On the day of the photo shoot and interview, I'll never forget *Ebony*'s photographer, Vandell Cobb, perching himself up on a stepladder to get an elevated shot of my brothers and sisters all huddled together, with my mom prominently positioned in the forefront. All of us were smiling, seemingly without a care in the world. Suddenly the camera man said, "Look up at the camera and smile," and then the camera flashed and that won-

Ebony photographer Vandell Cobb, (partially shown left) is perched up on ladder to take the photograph that appeared in the December 2006 issue of Ebony, page 141. Photo provided by Paul Hunter

derful moment of us together as a family was frozen in time forever.

Yes, that *Ebony* article was the first step in our national exposure, truly our first real fifteen minutes of fame. Monica Jones wrote an excellent story, and *Ebony* graciously gave her four pages to tell it. Imagine, four pages in *Ebony Magazine* which is a big breakthrough for an unknown publicist. Not only was this prestigious exposure in the African-American community, but *Ebony Magazine* has a well-established reputation as one of America's top magazines.

When Ebony hit the streets, I was surprised to find out that our story appeared in the December 2006 issue of Dream Girls with Beyoncé Knowles, Jennifer Hudson, and Anika Noni Rose on the cover. Beginning on page 140, there was a photograph of my mom out in front of her Mission, posing with her outstretched hands under the Love and Charity sign. The story title was "A Case of the Extraordinary." On page 140 was our group picture, with the word "Love" written in bold, bright red letters. Wow, those were all very good memories.

If you were to just look at the lovely photos published in *Ebony*, you might get the impression that we were all one big, cohesive, happy family. I mean, if you saw the picture, you would think we had it all together, that each of us was raised in a wholesome, loving environment, standing there behind our mother to support her. A large family should have a lot of love, right? She was a famous mom, a recognized and awarded humanitarian, who through adversity and trials beat the odds and had the tenacity and stamina to establish an urban mission. And more amazing still, she did it all while raising twenty-one children. You would think that we would be the very epitome of togetherness and familial love and support—but there's another side to this story. We were all accustomed to posing for the camera, and on the outside, you would never know that behind those gleaming eyes and bright smiles were years of painful neglect that all of my siblings experienced as part of the Hunter family.

If you look at the headlines characterizing my mother over the years, this is what you would see: "Mother To The World," *The Kinston Free Press*; "Extraordinary Life of Mother of 21," The *Los Angeles Sentinel*; "Giving Hope for 35 Years," *Milwaukee Journal Sentinel*; "Picture Having 21 Kids," *Milwaukee Journal Sentinel*; "Charity Begins at Home," *Today's Black Woman;* "A Case of the Extraordinary," *Ebony Magazine*; "The Heart of Love and Charity," *Today's Christian Magazine*; "Love In Abundance," *Upscale Magazine*; and "Meet Super Mom," *The National Examiner*. If you were to characterize my mother from those story titles alone, indeed you would walk away thinking, "Here's a person who walks on water." However, let me inform you that growing up a Hunter wasn't easy, and I can certainly attest that she doesn't walk on water. As a matter of fact, she wasn't a good mother at all.

Now don't get me wrong, my mother took care of us. She did things for us to live to become adults. She fed us and clothed us, and kept us with a roof over our heads, but what I'm saying is that there were two sides to her: the loving "super mom" image was her public persona, but the one that my brothers and sisters saw was the cold, detached woman who gave us the impression that she didn't want to be our mother. In fact, she didn't want us to even call her mother. We had to address her as "E," not Mommy, Ma' Dear, not Mom, but "E." When we were growing up none of us ever knew what "E" stood for, but as you read this book, it will become evident.

What symbolizes the nature of the relationship is the revelation of not being allowed to call her mother. Consequently, there are eighteen kids who have suffered from emotional neglect and abuse, who were sacrificed on the altar of a kingdom of her own making, the Love and Charity Homeless Shelter of Racine, Wisconsin.

This is why I am writing this book. Our life in public was a façade. We were not a happy family. Behind our gleaming eyes and bright smiles, there were dark family secrets lurking in the background, hidden from view until now. The truth is, I cannot remember the last time any of us were truly happy. With the lights and cameras and our prompted smiles, there were frowning hearts and broken spirits. Behind the bright, gleaming eyes were years of neglect, mental abuse, and cruelty, from the woman that outsiders called "Mother Hunter," but to us was simply E.

My mother—who was out to save the world, out

to help others' children—was cold and cruel to her own children. Yes, we participated in the lie because being in front of the camera and helping around the mission occasionally gave us joy and purpose, but at what cost? What were we going to do? We wanted a loving mother, a real mother, but the loving mother only existed for the camera, the lights, the newspaper articles, and the public. That sweet, loving, benevolent mother that the world saw never came home to us.

So, now I tell the story. This is how it really was, not the idealized account depicted in my mother's book *Love and Charity*, full of the half-truths that she spoon-fed to the author. Until now, no one but my brothers and sisters knew the real Hunter story. As you read this shocking but true account, realize that my brothers and sisters and I lived through—and some of us are still going through—the Hunter nightmare. Ironically, mother always saw her Mission as a beacon for love and charity which is why she named it Love and Charity. However, the reality belies the Love and Charity Homeless Shelter's name. Therefore, in telling the true story, I must name this book *No Love, No Charity: the Success of the 19th Child*.

Oddly, as much as my mother wanted to be successful and known, she never wanted to see any of her children become successful and known. We were never encouraged. We never felt loved and appreciated. Despite the emotionally toxic environment in which I was raised, I have survived, and I have confidence in my future success.

Undoubtedly, there will be some of my family members that will feel I should not be revealing the things that I do in this book. Their argument might be that these are family secrets and family business, not to be spoken about in a public forum. But to them I say, "The truth shall make you free." The Hunters lived in the public eye, and that's part of the problem: we were too public. While our matriarch mother was out saving the world, she was losing her own children through multilayered dysfunctions that were exacerbated by her need to be in the limelight and in control. Our family suffered, and many of my brothers and sisters who never had our mother's love, are still suffering to this day. It is my hope and prayer that the cycle of dysfunction like alcoholism, drug addiction, and illicit lifestyles will be broken once and for all.

CHAPTER 1

It Had Already Started

When I came into this world, I unwittingly stepped onto a production stage, a life pageant if you will, of my mother's own creation. In such a setting, she was the main attraction. She was the principal character, the rest of us just stage hands and extras. On page 84 of my mother's book, *Love and Charity*, there is a *Racine Journal Times* picture of my mother and my father, James Hunter, standing in front of her Love and Charity Club that she had just opened up. It was July 1, 1970. To the casual observer, you won't see me in the picture, but I'm there. Though it's not very obvious, my mother was wearing a maternity blouse because she was six months pregnant with me.

As I said, there has never been a time that I was not a part of her public life, but for many years I remained hidden behind the scenes, just as I was in that picture on Love and Charity's opening day. Three-and-a-half months later, on October 16, 1970, I was born. Ever since then, it has seemed to me as if I was born into adversity. The reason why I say into adversity is be-

Mrs. Moses Garcia, James Hunter, Louise Hunter
Photo by Chuck D' Acquisto, Racine Journal Times, 1970

cause my life has been full of difficulties, one trial after another, one tribulation after another, a routine that I have grown all too accustomed to ever since I was a child. I am the nineteenth child of twenty-one children, eighteen of us still living today. As I said earlier, my mother is the matriarch of a large clan, which includes sixty-one grandchildren and sixty-five great-grandchildren and counting.

My Father, James Hunter

With so many brothers and sisters, my earliest recollections of my family were hectic and chaotic. However, amidst all of the disarray and confusion, there were some fond memories, particularly of my father. In my opinion, James Hunter was a great man. My father was born in Fayetteville, Mississippi, in 1936. In the early 1950s, he and my mother met in Vicksburg, Mississippi, where they were married. When my dad met my mom, she already had three girls, Elizabeth, Seles, and Barbara Ann, and she was pregnant with my oldest brother, James Jr.

Years later, and even to this very day, my mother always claimed that James Jr. was dad's child, but he was not. He does not know who his real father is, and this has always inhibited his steps. Like a cancer, it ate away at him. I asked my brother, "Did my father ever say you were not his child?" He answered, "Yes. He used to say it to me all the time, especially when he disciplined me." My father knew, my brother knew, and, obviously, my mother knew the truth. Since my mom and dad were involved while she was already pregnant, my father gave him his name, hence James Jr. This was just an indicator of the type of man my father was. He knew the truth, but he stayed committed to the relationship. He loved my mother greatly, so he willingly took on the responsibility of raising Seles, Barbara Ann, and James Jr. Hunter. My sister Elizabeth was raised by my grandparents on my mother's side.

The way I understood it from my older siblings, James Hunter was a good provider. Early on in their relationship, my mother started having James' babies. With a growing family, they needed to leave Vicksburg to go to Kinston, North Carolina, to work in the tobacco fields. Eventually, Daddy got a job working for the city. However, my mother seemed to have a baby every year, and with his growing family, Daddy was forced to work two jobs to make enough money to make ends meet. In addition, there were the typical ups and downs that any married couple face, but Dad hung in there.

Even though my father had his good side, like anyone else, he had some shortcomings. At times Poppa could be a rolling stone. It wasn't that it was in his nature to be a rolling stone. It was the unrelenting pressure of family life, particularly the intense pressure my mother exerted. However, with all of that factoring into the equation, his shortcomings never negated his love and concern for us. He was genuinely compassionate, unlike my mother, who had a malicious streak that wouldn't quit.

My father was cool, calm, and collected. He had a great attitude. He was always laughing, smiling, and giving us a hug. He would let us sit on his lap and have a conversation with us. He was a very upbeat guy. He would talk to us and not yell. He was a straightforward guy. He would not sugarcoat anything whatsoever. This is the type of man he was. Unfortunately, I didn't have many years with him. I only had seven or eight years with him, and I enjoyed those years.

Dad's routine was to get up at five o'clock in the morning and go to work. He worked at the Case Tractor Plant in Racine, Wisconsin, Monday through Friday, but on the weekend, it was party time for him. Weekends were reserved for him, and there was nothing wrong with that. When you're working two jobs and you have a big family and you're working sixteen hours a day, you deserve the weekends. On Sundays, I vaguely remember Dad going to church. Sometimes he would go, but most times he would not. It depended on how he felt because church wasn't important to him. Although I never knew why, he didn't care too much about attending church. He was just going with the flow—that was his personality.

On the other hand, my mom never did have much of a personality, not even to this day. Around others, she portrayed a personality. That would be their first impression. Once they would get to know her, they would realize that she was pretending. She'd smile in your face but stab you in the back.

If you looked at my mother today and saw her conducting one of her worship services at the Mission, you would never know that at one time she was quite a reveler. She and my dad would go out to the local bars in Kinston and have a good time. As a matter of fact, my mother used to leave my brothers and sisters at home alone and run the street while my dad was at work. This is how my older sister Zollena was burned playing with the stove and started a fire that set the apartment ablaze. They lost their apartment and many of their possessions. Furthermore, Zollena almost lost her life. After that incident, my mom found religion, and the problems between Mom and Dad started.

Deep down inside, I believe my mother was trying to absolve herself of her previous irresponsibility by diving headlong into the church world. Almost overnight she became a religious zealot with a one-track mind. Maybe this sudden change was too much for my dad because one day he packed up his clothes and left my mother there in Kinston, heading back to Vicksburg. Eventually my mother followed him, and caught up with him in Vicksburg. After that, it wasn't long before they reconciled.

A few years after Zollena's fire tragedy and in search of a better life, my family moved to Racine, Wisconsin. My father had relatives in Racine, and that's where he, my mom and the kids stayed until they were able to find a place of their own. My mother never clicked with my dad's side of the family, and she never wanted us to have anything to do with them. I'm sure this was a bone of contention between my parents, one of many things they constantly argued about.

By the early 1960s, our family had grown to thirteen children. My mother was pregnant with my older brother Larry, the fourteenth child, when an incident occurred that changed the destiny of the Hunter family. According to the story, during the winter season, a deputy sheriff's officer knocked on the door and served my mom with an eviction notice. Apparently, word had gotten back to the landlord that fifteen people (thirteen kids and Mom and Dad) were living in a two-bedroom apartment. Citing occupancy violations, they gave my mom thirty days to find a new place. When the thirty days were up, the sheriff returned. My family was still present. They had nowhere to go, so my mom requested one more day. The next day a miracle happened, and a stranger showed up and gave our family an eighteen-room house for the price of one dollar which the man paid himself.

It wasn't long after this benevolent intervention that my mother decided to start helping others. In theory, returning the act of kindness shown to us seemed to be the thing to do. None of us knew at that defining moment in our lives what this really would mean for the Hunter family. We would have to make sacrifices while E pursued her dreams, a dream that included us, but not by choice.

As the years passed, my mother kept having a baby every year for twenty years. The strain of our ever bigger family put tremendous pressure on my dad, and it seemed like whatever my father did wasn't enough. By now, my mom had turned *super*—or should I say *superficially*—religious which added a lot of tension in the house. None of us were ever right enough, especially my dad. He caught the brunt of it for a long time.

My father had to work two or even three jobs, but my mom never worked outside the home. I guess having my brothers and sisters was reason enough, but instead of being supportive, my mother had her own agenda. I remember that my father and mother argued frequently because my mother used to take the hard-earned dollars that my father would bring home—the money that was needed to buy food and clothes for us—and give it to the preacher. Unfortunately, E believed that if she gave the money to the preacher, God would provide another miracle as he had with the first house.

Therefore, my mother wouldn't pay the utilities. In her defense, she would always say that God would provide. However, my mother never seemed to be able to come to grips with the fact that not only did God want believers to pay tithes, but He also wanted them to pay their bills, not ignore them.

In the Hunter family, Sunday was a big day. It started off with us going to church. As a kid, I enjoyed church services sometimes, but most times I did not because I didn't understand what was happening. I was too young to understand the concept of the preaching, the teaching, the screaming, and the deliverance stuff. I used to sit back and wonder, "What is going on?" In retrospect, the church environment was not the best environment for a child like me to be in. The progressive churches had children's church, geared towards teaching the Bible in a way that's understandable for children. However, the church my mother attended didn't have that, so we had to struggle to understand. We didn't have a choice in the matter; like it or not, we had to attend church.

Just imagine the fight it was getting us up in the mornings. It is difficult to get one child up for school or church; multiply that by nineteen, and you get the picture. However, I enjoyed every bit of it. Sundays were church. After church the pastor would sometimes come over for a big meal with the family. It was a tradition in the African-American community for the pastor to preach and then accept an invitation to someone's house for a huge Sunday dinner.

One Sunday as a child, I remember the pastor came to our house. My mother and my dad prepared fried chicken. She had corn, chocolate cake, caramel cake, sweet potato pie, and greens for the pastor. The pastor looked forward to that Sunday. When he was in our house, I remember that he sat at the head of the table. Keep in mind, the head of the table was supposed to be my father's spot, but when the pastor came, he took the head of the table. The pastor would say the prayer and was served first before any children and any adults. This is what I remember about Sunday mornings—going to church, praising the Lord, going back home, and running around the house while Mom and Dad prepared the food. I was just a typical kid who had a lot of energy. I enjoyed it.

At times, Sunday mornings were a fight for Mom to get Dad to go to church or for her to get Dad to help us get dressed for church. At first I didn't like getting up on Sunday mornings, but once my siblings and I got up and the energy kicked in, we were ready to go to church. That was a typical Sunday for the Hunter family. After church, we knew there was going to be a big meal. It was happy time. Sunday evening was our happy meal. It would put a smile on our faces to have a big "happy meal" Sunday dinner.

Those were some of the wholesome times and activities that occurred on Sunday in the Hunter home. To this day, I miss Sunday soul food. I wish I could relive my childhood because I would love to have the joyous atmosphere with all my brothers and sisters and my mom and dad together again.

Although I didn't like going to church, I enjoyed the food. After we ate, we would go outside and run it off. That's what kids do best, playing and burning off energy.

Unfortunately, Sunday, the fun day, was only one day a week. The rest of the week could be characterized as being contentious. During that period in our lives, the relationship between my mother and father was very tense. E constantly put my dad down. She had something negative to say, one put-down after the other, one criticism after the other. When she wasn't at home fussing with us or my dad, she was running around Racine trying to keep her precious Love and Charity Club going. E was concerned about the mission, and nothing came before Love and Charity, not my brothers, my sisters, and certainly not my father. My father tried compromising with my mom by chipping in to help her with Love and Charity. This is why they are pictured together on Love and Charity's opening day. My father and brothers and sisters even helped out with the choir, but most of the time we took a back seat to the mission, and, even more humiliating, we took a back seat to the transients that E brought to the house. This would infuriate my dad to no end. Strangers were sleeping in our beds and eating our food while we were required to make the sacrifice for what my mom called "the Lord's work."

Due to my mother's work, the miracle eighteen-room house that started out as a haven of rescue for a distressed, oversized family became a magnet for the city's undesirables, who often freeloaded at our expense. It continued like that, day in and day out, but little did my mother or any of us know that a tragedy was lurking around the corner. Once again, my mother left home and left us inadequately supervised which set the stage for tragedy to strike. This time it had deadly results.

The Death of My Brother Thomas

It was February 27, 1976, and my mom left home to do "the Lord's work." My brothers Timothy, Gregory, Thomas, and I were taking advantage of the fact that E wasn't at home. We actually enjoyed it when E wasn't there because we could rabble-rouse throughout the house. We didn't play too much in the house when our mother was around because she would get angry at the drop of a hat and beat our butts. E would use a belt or hit us in the face with a shoe if we upset her. We were all afraid of E. Anyway, my brother got hold of some matches and a gas can and ended up setting that miracle house on fire. The place practically burned to the ground. We barely escaped with our lives.

To this day I can still remember two firemen coming to rescue my brother and me. I was terrified, yelling out for my mom and dad, so one of the firemen grabbed me. I then looked over at Thomas and saw the other fireman was trying feverishly to revive him. He checked my brother's pulse and said to the fireman that was holding me, "His pulse is very weak. I don't think he's going to make it." He then tried giving my brother some oxygen.The other fireman said, "We have to get out of here now." He grabbed my brother, and we fought our way out of that smoky room. Fire was everywhere,

The miracle house ablaze. Photo by Arthur P. Haas,
Racine Journal Times, Racine Wis., 1976

raging around us, in the bedrooms and consuming the stairs. It felt like we were in a furnace.

Leaving the second floor was dangerous because the stairs had been weakened by the fire. When we got downstairs, much of the first floor was engulfed. Fire was coming out of the kitchen and the living room. In order to get us out of the house safely, the fireman grabbed a garbage can that my mother used to store flour and sugar in, took the lid off of the trash can, and poured the contents out on the floor. He then put my brother and me into that garbage can, put the lid back on and safely brought us through the flames. They rushed my brother and me to the hospital. It was too late for Thomas, who succumbed to smoke inhalation and died a day or so later.

It's funny how my mother always told the tale that a stranger darted into the house and placed me in a large can and rescued me from the fire. It's even in her book, but that didn't happen. It was the firemen who rescued me and my brother.

By this time, my dad had almost completely dropped out of our family scene. Between homeless folks living in our house, my mother running the streets doing "the Lord's work" and giving the money to the preachers in town, my dad saw no use in coming home some nights, so during the tragedy, Daddy was on one of his hiatuses, and my mother was busy being Racine's Mother Teresa. She had appearances and an image to keep up. Hardly anyone outside our family was wise to what was really going on with the Hunters behind closed doors.

The tragic fire was covered by the news. Pictures of our blazing home were even published in the *Racine Journal Times* and in my mother's biography on pages 96 and 98. The town was shocked, and everyone felt sorry for the Hunters. By this time, my family was well known in Racine for my mother's work at her Love and Charity organization.

The funeral for Thomas was well attended. The mayor of Racine and several city officials, including the firemen that rescued my brothers and sisters, were in attendance. I remember the funeral service was crowded. The community came to support the Hunter family. The firemen who rescued us even spoke at my brother's funeral. The community opened up to us and embraced us in this difficult time. Yes, Racine's citizenry was good to us after the fire tragedy. We went back to life as usual, but now we moved to a house on Hamilton Street.

For a brief while, my mom and dad made peace long enough to get back together again as we mourned the loss of Thomas. Ironically, no one ever put my parents, particularly my mom, under the microscope for leaving children at home alone. It's true that she asked my older brother Michael to supervise us. Technically, he was old enough to be left at home to watch us, but the real issue was that this was the norm. E always put Love and Charity before her own children and my father.

E was often somewhere else, but not with us. We all hated the fact that we had to share our mother with everyone else while we got the leftovers. We knew it, but we had to deal with it because we couldn't change it. This was the life of living in the shadows of E and her Love and Charity work.

After Thomas' death, it put a lot of pressure on my mom and dad. They used to argue and blame each other because my mom was at church, and my dad was out when it happened. My dad blamed my mom because he had told her not to go to church. He wanted her to stay home. There was a lot of confusion and fighting when we moved to Hamilton Street. When a death enters into a person's home, I believe that if you are not spiritually fit for the test, you will depart and separate from each other. My father and mother just grew apart. When we moved into our new home, there was only fighting and turmoil between them, a bitter wedge that eventually drove them apart.

Whenever my mother did not want to be around, she would claim she was going to church. Going to church or doing the Lord's will was her convenient excuse for being MIA. "I can't do this or that because I'm doing the Lord's will," is what she would always say. As you would expect, my brothers and sisters and I couldn't say much about this because we were just children. However, I'm sure that brought a division into the home between my dad and mom.

That Late Night Cup of Coffee

The relationship between my mother and father continued to decline. E wasn't at home. What my mother was really doing was abdicating her responsibilities as a mother and wife by hanging out at the church. The members of the local church that she attended didn't know my mother was a hypocrite. She used to shout at church all the time, "Hallelujah! Hallelujah! Thank you,

Jesus! Thank you, Jesus! But while she was shouting, she was taking the Lord's name in vain because she was a hypocrite behind closed doors.

After a while, my father questioned E's so-called church involvement. Suspiciously my dad would ask, "Are you doing the Lord's work?" He would ask this because he knew that after church was over, my mother still wouldn't come home. Instead of returning to her family, E would be out having coffee with the preachers.

Yes, my "holier than thou" mother, when finished with church, would go out with the ministers for coffee until two or three in the morning. Something was up with that. My father couldn't understand it, and he didn't believe it. I believe his suspicions were right. There had to be more than caffeine that was stimulating my mother, and my dad knew it. Poppa may have been a rolling stone at times himself, but he wasn't a fool. When you are out that late with another man, supposedly "having coffee," preacher or not, that opens the door to rumor and speculation.

Daddy Leaves but Never Returns

Well, enough was enough. Though my father tried his best to cope with my mom's antics and fanaticism, given his weaknesses, it simply became too much for him to handle. One statement after another of constantly putting him down had taken its toll. My mother's late nights out with other men eroded any hope of mending the relationship. Besides, my mother verbally beat my father down. She verbally beat us all down.

My mother had a way with words. Words were her weapons even though she is functionally illiterate and has a very limited vocabulary. However, what words she did have were used like daggers. Her words were like vials of poison to be poured onto our dysfunctional hearts, where the only thing that could grow was low self-esteem, self-loathing, despondency, and hopeless-

James Hunter (1936-1978)
Photo provided by Patrick Hunter, I Come 2 U Photo

ness. These were the corrupt seeds that cultivated our hurting family. Her words were words of criticism and castigation. Very rarely did we hear an encouraging word. When my mother got through with us, we felt worthless and hopeless.

After taking years of abuse from my mother, my father threw in the towel and decided enough was enough. My dad got sick and tired of it, including her physical abuse. I remember when my dad left. I was outside playing with my brothers Timothy, Gregory, and my nephew Anthony. We were little kids having a good time. My dad called each of us to the car. He said to us, "I love you, but I can't take this anymore." He gave us a hug and a kiss. I didn't know then that it would be the last time I was going to see him alive.

Dad left for Mississippi. The gist of what he was saying was tearfully simple: "I can't deal with your mother anymore." He had reached the point of no return. His broken heart and spirit finally succumbed to the unrelenting verbal abuse and pressure from my mother.

A few days later, after the long drive to Fayetteville, Mississippi, my father arrived at his mother's house. He visited with his mom for a little while and then decided to leave. His mom asked him what he was going to do that night. He said he was going out to see some friends and relatives. He was going out partying. However, my grandma told him not to go. "Stay here with me. I haven't seen you in years," she insisted. However, Dad said no, that he'd rather go out for a while. My father got into his car and left.

After going a mile or so down the road, he pulled up and stopped at a red light at a four-way intersection. Once the light changed, he proceeded. He was hit broadside in a horrific collision by an RV. The RV driver wasn't paying attention and had run the red light. The car was mangled, and Daddy was barely clinging to his life. After he was transported to the hospital, he was immediately listed in critical condition. They put him on life support. After a few days of my father lingering in intensive care, my mother gave the doctors her consent to take him off life support. Shortly after, he passed away.

They brought his body back to Racine to prepare him for the funeral. It was a sad funeral. Friends and relatives got up and spoke about what a great person he was and testified as to how he had impacted their lives. Yes, my dad influenced a lot of people's lives, especially those of his children, who now had to grow up without him. That was a hard thing for us. It was difficult because every child deserves both parents, in spite of how they may feel about them.

After my dad was laid to rest, my brother Gregory asked my mother about my father's gravesite, but my mother wouldn't give him any information. That was unbelievable. However, with or without my mother's cooperation, Gregory was determined to find Dad's grave, and as an adult he did. The intriguing thing that he discovered was that the day my father passed away is now his own wedding anniversary date. Another weird coincidence was that the suit my father bought to wear to my brother Thomas' funeral was the same suit he died in two years later, not having worn that suit in between. That was an eerie coincidence.

We never fully understood why we couldn't get information from E about our father. We've always wanted to know, what went wrong? Why did Daddy up and leave? Though we tried, to this day we still haven't been able to get any information. She will take that information to her grave. She claims she is a Christian and loves the Lord and would do anything for the Lord, but how cold could she be to her family? All I can say is that the death of my brother Thomas and the death of my father James Hunter were very traumatic tragedies that changed our lives.

Unlike Gregory, I have never been to my father's gravesite. Someday I will go. When I do, I will take a photo and share it with the world. Seeing his final resting place will bring some necessary closure, but maybe that's why I still haven't gone. I am not ready for closure. My dad was good to me and my siblings. I never had a problem with my dad. He died, at forty-two, a young man.

When I was a young man, I used to wonder if I would live longer than my father. By the time this book gets released, I guess I'll have my answer. Because on October 16, 2012, Lord willing, I'll be forty-two years old. Even though I haven't quite gotten there yet, I already know that it's too young to die. I hope by the grace of God that I will live long enough to see my grandkids walk this earth.

CHAPTER 2

My Brothers and Sisters

My father's death was a hard one, particularly coming only two years after we buried Thomas. It was hard for the Hunters. We had to deal with all of that hurt. It seemed like my dad had been my only ally, but now he was gone. As a child, I grew up bitter and angry at the world because I saw other kids enjoying ample time with their fathers. I was a pot of bitterness, just waiting for the opportunity to lash out at anyone.

With the pain that I was carrying from my father's death and the cruel detachment from my mother, I began to act out in school. I was eight years old and I was in the third grade. Oddly, my mother knew I was troubled, but it never seemed to register with her. It would have been obvious to a caring, loving mother, but E was focused on everything else but her children. My mother never knew why some of my brothers and sisters were heading down the wrong road, becoming delinquent.

We were all troubled one way or another. However, instead of seeing our negative behaviors as a cry for help, E only castigated us further. This was like pouring salt on an open wound. It was truly adding insult to injury. We weren't asking for much. We weren't asking for any more than what any other children would need from parents—to be loved, supported, and validated. We wanted to be respected and appreciated. That's all we needed, but instead my mother beat us into the ground with her words. Instead of building up our self-esteem, she systematically destroyed it, piece by piece.

We were a talented sibling group. We had potential. My brothers and sisters should have been doctors, lawyers, judges, and athletes. They should have been famous, great humanitarians who could have made a great impact on the world. None of us saw the light of possibility and hope because we were forced to live in the shadows of Louise Hunter and Love and Charity.

As children, we did not have a great life. We were poor. We struggled. We went without, but we were family. You have to understand that when you come from a big family, you are going to have some fights and arguments with your sisters and brothers. It's a part of life. I learned a lot from my sisters and brothers, from both the good and the bad. I learned from some of their mistakes. That's why I say that experience is not always the best teacher. We can learn from one another's mistakes. I don't have to experience crack cocaine for myself to know that it will destroy a life.

Other than the extraordinary number of them, my sisters and brothers are like any other sibling group. At times we did things that were inappropriate, as children do. Nevertheless, I love my sisters and brothers. I don't play favorites, but I appreciate their uniqueness and individuality.

Elizabeth, my oldest sister, is the typical oldest child. She acts like the commander-in-chief. She looks like Chaka Khan. She's an entertainer, a go-getter, and she has an entrepreneurial spirit. She goes and gets what she needs. That's a mind-set that I have always admired.

My sister Seles is a great cook. I love conversing with her. She's a straight-up woman who will tell you the truth. She will not sugarcoat anything at all.

My sister Barbara Ann can have an attitude, but that's okay. I understand that. She always has had an attitude, ever since I was a child. But the thing that I love the best about Barbara Ann is that she can cook fried chicken. "Barbara Ann," I would say, "when I become rich, I'm going to hire you to cook and clean for me."

My brother James is a character. James is a precise person. He doesn't say much. He's a jolly guy. He's not a communicator. When he talks, he wants to be short and move on to the next subject which is fine with me.

Bonnie is the family diva. When she dresses up, you'd better watch out. Once she dresses up, guys go crazy over her. They would say my sister is gorgeous.

My sister Zollena is nice. She is kind, sweet, and will do anything for people. She's a person who will take the shirt off her back and give it to you to help you out. She's a helper. She would do anything to see you make progress in life.

My sister Jacqueline will listen to you and offer advice. She will communicate with you. Whatever you talk about will stay a secret. She will not inform anyone of the conversation that you had with her. Jacqueline is constantly on the move. One minute she's in Racine for six months to a year. The next minute she's in Minnesota. She just comes and goes.

My sister Sonja is pretty. Guys would chase after her. She's a soft-spoken person, but a go-getter. She likes to relax. She likes to stay active. She fits in no matter where she goes, blending into any situation or environment. She is not a problem child; however, she and my mom never got along. I believe my mom may have been jealous of her beauty.

My sister Connie likes to enjoy life. She loves people and has a gentle spirit, but she is strong-willed. She'll say, "Hey, we're not doing it this way. We will do it this way." That's the way she is, and there is nothing wrong with having that attitude.

My brother Patrick vacillates. If you had two candidates running to be the president of the United States, and Patrick was listening to the Republican speak, after he finished speaking, Patrick would say, "I'm going to vote for him." Then when the Democratic candidate finished his speech, Patrick would say, "No, I'm going with the Democrat." Patrick can't make a decision. Although indecisive, Patrick is a good man.

My brother Larry has always been hard-nosed. "You are going to do what I tell you to do or get out." He has a tough mentality. There is nothing wrong with having a tough mentality when you grew up in a tough neighborhood like we did. Larry is a leader. He's a leader in his home, in church, and in the kingdom of God. He has started an alcohol and drug addiction rehabilitation home in Memphis and is a pastor of a growing church. He is walking a similar road that my mother walked in that he has a desire to help hurting people, but that's the only thing they have in common. Larry is kind and genuinely concerned about helping the disenfranchised. Despite my mother doing many hurtful things to Larry, he hasn't let her venom poison his life, and I know he will go on to accomplish great things.

My brother Michael is constantly on the move. It's like he's running from something, and I wonder what that is. He's a goodhearted guy, and he is talented. He plays the bass and the drums. As he gets older, he's going to realize he's wasted a lot of time running because you can't run from yourself. Hopefully he will come back where he started, and come to grips with who God called him to be. I hope it will be soon.

My brother Calvin is Mr. Big Time in the Family. He is the athlete in the family. He was known as the ladies' man when he was younger. Now he is known as the brilliant cook. If he is in the kitchen, let him dictate how he wants the food prepared. My brother is worse than Gordon Ramsay of Hell's Kitchen.

My brother Timothy is chasing the world these days. Timothy's character is wacked out. One minute he's going north. The next minute he's going south. He's a fast talker. He'll get all over you. That little sucker knows the street game. If he catches you slipping, he's got you. He reminds me of some people in New York City. With his fast talk, when he gets through with you, he has already convinced you to give him some money. Then he's gone to the next victim. See you later, alligator. Then you realize, "I just got beat. What should I do?"

My brother Gregory is a choirboy who wants to feel like he's in a gang. It seems like he has something to prove to his friends. "I'm tough. I'm hard." Yet, when you peel off the layers, you'll discover that he's not hard. He's needs to be loved. His talents need to be exposed. He needs to believe in himself and in God. He needs to say, "Who cares what my friends say? Who cares what my relatives or associates say? I am changing." He has to be the leader that God has called him to be. He has to understand that whatever has happened in the past, he needs to leave the past behind and move on. He's a goodhearted person, but sometimes he gets lured back into that "I'm a gangbanger. I'm a player. I'm good-looking."

My sister Elsie reminds me of the story of Moses in the Bible. Moses was in the wilderness with his people for about forty years, but he was not allowed to go into the Promised Land. He was only allowed to see it. Elsie is in the wilderness. I believe that God is going to do something in her life. She constantly sucks her thumb. I remember when I was driving with my buddy, and he said, "Hey, man, look at that girl. She has got her thumb in her mouth." I turned around and said, "Man, that's my sister Elsie, and she's been doing that ever since she was a child." No matter what she's doing, she is sucking her thumb. He said, "She is too old to be sucking her thumb." I just laughed. Elsie has to be Elsie.

Last but not least is my baby sister Lashonda. She is the twenty-first child. You want to talk about a character? She likes to use profanity. You have to be prepared for her. She is the type of person who will tell you off in a minute. She is not afraid to fight you. Some people don't like that about her. She's a gifted woman.

All of my brothers and sisters have weaknesses. Some of my brothers and sisters like to drink, smoke weed, or do drugs. This is the life that they have decided to live. Adults make decisions as to how they are going to live—make the decisions, live with the consequences.

In spite of my brothers' and sisters' weaknesses and strengths, failures and victories, I love them for who they are. I know that there is something better for them. I am experiencing it right now. What's out there for me is out there for them too. I have a relationship with God because that's what I discovered. In spite of what other people think, people need a relationship with God. That's how my siblings are going to become successful. They are going to realize that they tried everything they can, and they don't have any results. Once they step their foot into the church and the body of Christ, they will get blessings and they will remain there, living the life that God called them to live.

I blame my mother and her seeds of despair for the hopelessness and self-destruction that my siblings and I have experienced. Among my siblings, there is a lot of drug and alcohol abuse. There is mental illness, depression, suicide attempts, divorce and the inability to maintain meaningful relationships. There has been incarceration and multigenerational substance abuse. All of this occurred in the background of my mother putting on the façade of saving the world and doing "the Lord's work."

I'm not claiming to be better than anyone else, but it is a shame to see how E's unbalanced commitment to Love and Charity contributed to the deterioration and destruction of many of my siblings. From their late 30s to their early 60s, they still seek validation from her, a validation she dangles like a carrot on a stick. She lets them get close enough to again verbally smash them into the ground. The fact is, my mother does not care about her own children; she's all about what they can do for her. If they can't do anything for her or the mission which is an extension of her, they can get out of her face. I must say I don't want anything bad to happen to my mom. As messed up as she is and we all are, we still love her. She's our mother, the only mother we have. All we ever wanted was her love, something she could never manage to give us.

To those reading this book, you may get the impression that I loathe my mother. I don't—I love her. My family and I want to see her set free from all of the dysfunction that has insidiously crept down through our generations. Sickness breeds sickness. Dysfunction promotes more dysfunction and despondency. Although I harbor no ill will against my mother, I dislike her wicked ways, ways the public never sees. That's why I'm speaking out now. It will be cathartic for myself and my siblings.

Healing is a good thing. However, the only way healing can occur is with the light of the truth. For a lie to have power it must lurk in the dark shadows. This is why John 8:32 says, "The truth shall make you free." Unfortunately, my mother would often misquote the Bible. The devil is the father of all lies. My mother used lies to control and manipulate us and anyone else she wanted to control. Unfortunately, the Love and Charity Homeless Shelter gave my mother a powerful platform of influence to wield the power she coveted. My mother was good at concealing secrets and perpetuating falsehoods. Truth brings healing into the family, and healing is what the Hunter family has always needed most.

CHAPTER 3

The School Years

After my father died, things became very tight for us financially. We were barely making it. We were dirt poor, and it seemed like our mother, now without a husband and without income, was taking us through some terrible times, trying to survive. We didn't have beds, not even a mattress. We were sleeping on cold hardwood floors. Sometimes food was scarce, and even if there was enough food, there were times that there weren't enough plates, bowls, or silverware. One morning all of my siblings ate cold breakfast cereal out of one big pot. It was every kid for himself. Whoever scooped and ate the fastest, ate the most. Needless to say, there were many mornings we went to school hungry.

When we made it to school, it could be very humiliating because it was obvious that we were poor. My classmates didn't hold back from teasing and laughing at us. We were often referred to as the nasty Hunters, but that didn't stop us from loving one another. Though things were tight and often hectic, our lives were still punctuated with good memories. We had a big home, but struggled with having less of everything. We had less, but it brought out the best in us because we learned to improvise, share, and be a team. I'm telling you, less can be best. We had to share our clothes. One day Gregory would wear this uniform. The next day Timothy would wear Gregory's uniform while I would wear Timothy's uniform that he had worn the day before. It rotated. Sometimes we wore mix-matched socks. I did not care about that. It really brought us closer together, sharing a toothbrush, clothes, and food.

Though children are usually unaware of their family's economic status, being hungry was a terrible thing to experience. Sometimes we would come home from school hungry, and other times we would have to tolerate eating the same food every day. Usually what we ate was pinto beans and cornbread. If we didn't happen to have beans and cornbread, we would have biscuits and syrup. My mom's biscuits would stick to your stomach. This was all that we had. The world should know that we were dirt poor, but I say all of this because we could have been living better than what we were. My mother never wanted to get educated and learn a trade or anything like that so that she could provide adequately for her family.

Had my mother not been set against education, I believe she could've gone a lot further in life. Look at what my mother accomplished with hardly any education. Ironically, my mother used to say, "The Lord gives me the knowledge, and the Lord gives me wisdom." As a child I constantly heard this, so I thought God was just going to come down, open up my head, and pour in wisdom and knowledge. For a long time I thought that's how it worked, but it didn't take long for me to learn that was absolutely false. God does not do that at all. I sought to educate myself, and with the Lord's help and hard work, I now have my bachelor's degree.

As I look back at all the negative criticisms my

mother had about education and those who are educated, I understand that these were all excuses for not
wanting to go back to school herself. The truth is my
mother is functionally illiterate. My mother doesn't know
simple things like how a sentence is to be constructed.
If you asked her what are the elements of a sentence: a
subject and a predicate—she wouldn't know. Nor would
she know that a sentence expresses a complete thought.
The only emphasis my mom placed on anything was to
claim that God called her to do this or that. Unfortunately, as a child, I didn't know any better. I thought all
of what she was saying was true.

In addition to my mother's issues with the classroom, she also had a problem with us playing any type
of sports. She would always make up excuses whenever
it was time to take us to get physical exams, a prerequi-
site in order to be considered for any of the teams. She
would always use the same lame excuse: I can't take you
to the doctor because I have to do the Lord's will. Even
when my mother was supposed to come to school for
parent-teacher conferences, my mom would not show
up. When the school called home and spoke to Mom, she
would tell them that she couldn't come because she had
to do the Lord's work. Everything she had to do was all
about the Lord, but it was never about our family. My
mother mastered shirking her parental responsibilities
in favor of a self-imposed higher calling where she
served God, but it was a god of her own making, who
was only concerned with mindless and heartless service
from people like my mother.

As I grew older, it became clear to me why my
mother was actually against the idea of being educated.
At first I thought it was just due to the fact that while
she was being raised in the Deep South back during the
1930s, young blacks often had to work the cotton fields
during planting and harvest season, having little chance
of being educated. Consequently, my mom can barely
read and write. However, in 1970 when I was born,

times had changed considerably for blacks, and though racial issues hadn't gone away, things were much better compared to when my mother was growing up. I was curious about everything. I wanted to know how the world worked. I wanted to improve my communication skills. I wanted to grow intellectually just as I was growing physically. However, my mom was against the whole idea and played down the benefits of education. She felt if you needed to know something, the Lord would teach you. Such a superstitious attitude toward education was baseless. It was indicative of years of conditioning that black people should be subservient and dependent upon their master, even if the master was a blond-haired picture of Jesus in a dingy gold-colored frame. I have never seen a picture of Jesus with blue eyes!

Since my grandparents were sharecroppers, it is a good possibility that they were born close to the turn of the twentieth century if not before. Sharecropping was a way to keep blacks subservient to their former slave owners after slavery was abolished. During slavery, it was illegal to educate blacks. To teach a slave to read or write could mean severe punishment or even death. Generations of blacks equated education with something terrible, something to protect your children against. In order to survive, a slave mother would chastise her own children for even thinking of the idea of learning to read and write. After hundreds of years of this type of conditioning and decades of brutal Jim Crow segregation after slavery, there are many blacks from my mother's generation that still have negative feelings towards education, even though there was no longer a basis for that fear. As we now all know, education is the great liberator.

Elementary School: Illegitimately Labeled

Like most people, I have some fond memories of my elementary school years. I attended two elementary schools in Racine, Wisconsin: Roosevelt and Janes elementary. Though elementary school played a very important role in my early education, being in the classroom also provided a welcome social setting and a break from my often chaotic home environment. For the most part, when I was in attendance, I enjoyed school. But there were many days that I never left home because E would keep me at home. Why? Because it was part of a game that my mother played in order to game the system. As a result, instead of learning reading, writing, and arithmetic, I was being taught how to be dishonest and get money from the government.

Unfortunately, it was my mother who encouraged me to be dishonest. I can remember that E told me to lie about why I wasn't attending school. I remember skipping school to go to the Social Security office with my mother. She told me to be dishonest about my mental functioning and capacity. All too often, African-American children are mislabeled and misdiagnosed with learning disabilities (LD). During that time, it seemed like it was normal for a lot of the black kids in the elementary school to receive LD status. Although there were academic interventions put in place for kids with special needs, like specialized curriculums tailored for children with these types of disabilities, there was also a financial benefit for that diagnosis. Whenever a school determined that the child had a learning disability, that family was eligible to receive Supplemental Security Income (SSI) payments which meant a few hundred dollars a month because of the child's diagnosis.

My mother prompted me and rehearsed me on how to act as if I were mentally challenged for the SSI evaluators. My mom told me to act like I was dumb or *retarded* (as they called it back then). I remember specifically going to the psychologist's office for evaluation and my mother saying, "I need you to act up. Act like you can't read. Act like you can't write. Act like you can't speak well. If he gives you anything like a pencil, act like it is something to play with or grab it and throw it on the floor immediately or break it." Then she would put the responsibility on me by saying, "You have to act up good because we need this money."

So, I would go into the psychologist's office to get evaluated and do those things that she had rehearsed with me. I was being deceptive with my mother's approval. I knew how I was acting wasn't true, but E told me to do it. I was a kid just doing what his momma told him to do. Unfortunately, the dishonesty that was validated by my mother started a pattern of dishonesty in my life. Some of my siblings have used the same dishonest tactics with their children, gaming SSI. It's a multi-generational how-to-game-the-system, with the side effects of children being inappropriately labeled and growing up dependent upon the system. Unfortunately, these diagnoses can follow you for life.

My mother also encouraged me to be dishonest with school officials as well. For whatever reason, my mother would keep me out of school. However, if I didn't go to school, I would eventually get a visit from the truant officer. My mom used to always say, "When the school sends that person to do that home visit and see if you're really sick, you lay down on the couch, put a blanket over you and say that you are sick." I was being obedient to my mother but dishonest with the truant officer. I mean, what kid wouldn't stay home from school with his or her mom's permission and tell a parentally sanctioned lie to stay home?

Now I see what E was doing with me as a child. She was a parent planting a seed in me to lie. She was preparing me to take dangerous, dishonest shortcuts in life that could only lead to disaster. What loving mother teaches her kids how to lie and get one over on the system, a path that is sure to lead that child to destruction? Greed and ignorance are a devastating combination with long-lasting effects.

Whenever dishonesty is encouraged in the home,

it's not long before other negative behaviors begin to surface in school. I remember one incident that occurred while at Roosevelt Elementary School was when my sister Elsie, my nephew Matthew, a friend of mine named J.C. Mosley and I got into trouble for beating up a kid during recess. The teacher wrote a blue slip and gave it to the principal. Mr. Margosian spanked us on our behinds. I remember going into the office, and he had all four of us in there. He said, "I just called your parents and informed them that I'm going to spank you guys. We're going to start with you, Paul. You first." I had to bend over while he took a paddle and spanked me three times. I started crying. He said, "Have a seat. Elsie, you're next." Elsie started crying after he hit her three times.

Then he hit Matthew three times, and he started crying. Last but not least, the principal spanked J.C. Mosley. J.C. was a big kid. He was about a good two hundred twenty-five pounds. He bent over. The principal hit him the first time, and Elsie, Matthew, and I started to laugh uncontrollably. Mr. Margosian said to us, "If you guys laugh at him, I'm going to spank all of you again." So he hit J.C. the second time, and we didn't laugh. He hit J.C. the third time, and I burst out laughing. He said, "Paul, come here." He hit me three more times. I cried like a baby. I learned my lesson, to keep my hands to myself. I said I'd never do that again. When we went home, E tore our butts up, whipping us with an extension cord. Whether she used an extension cord or what we in the African-American community called a "switch" (a small thin tree or bush limb), the beatings were very painful and left welts on our skin.

Many have wondered why so many black people have whipped their children in this way, particularly if you had parents who were baby-boomers and older. The answer has historic roots. The mentality of disciplinary brutality was born out of the Jim Crow and slavery eras, a period where blacks were beaten into submission for anything their masters thought they did wrong. "If they are disobedient, beat it out of them." Behavior can be controlled with a whip. People who were raised out of that period, like my mother whose parents were share-croppers (an institution of servitude instituted after the Emancipation), had a "beat it out of them" mentality. Though brutality comes in all races, colors, and creeds, it was ingrained in our people after hundreds of years of chattel slavery. Now that I'm old enough, I understand the mind-set and the ignorance behind this type of bru-tal corporal punishment, and I can say that I would never do that to my children.

After that whole ordeal, E would say, "If you go back to school and do that again, you are really gonna get it." I was afraid of E's extension cord although she was known for hitting you with whatever was available, whether it be a shoe or whatever. You didn't want E hitting on you. When we returned to school the next day, we were further punished by not being allowed to go out-side for recess. For an elementary school kid, that was cruel and unusual punishment. This whole experience taught me a great lesson, one that I will never forget.

I also remember an incident that occurred when I transferred from Roosevelt Elementary to attend Janes Elementary School. When I made that transfer I did not like the environment there nor the students. No matter how hard I tried, I just couldn't fit in. I remember asking my teacher Mrs. Jan, "Can I go use the bathroom?" When I went to go use the bathroom, I went in there to cry. A teacher came in and heard me crying. She took me to the office. I was crying uncontrollably. They called my mother. She got on the phone and did not have the soft tone of a loving mother who was concerned about a child in distress.

She said to me, "Boy, what are you crying for?" I said, "I want to go back to Roosevelt." No sir, I didn't like Janes Elementary School at all, but I had to adapt to the situation. The principal spoke to me. I calmed down and went home. I remember when I walked in the door at 709 Hamilton Street, some of my older sisters and brothers and some young ones were waiting for me. They were ready to tease me because my mother had informed them of what had happened. I remember my brother Gregory mocking me, "I want to go back to Roosevelt." They were all laughing. My brothers and sisters tortured me for a good month. They mocked me. Not only didn't my mother cuddle me, she turned my siblings loose on me with their endless teasing. That situation left a lasting impression on my mind.

Though my elementary schools years were characterized by misdiagnosis and manipulation, there were some positive experiences too. I managed to get through it and finally made it to middle school.

Middle School

One of the things I remember about attending Jerstad Agerholm middle school is that it was difficult because we were in transition. Since I was a troubled young man, living in the shadows of a domineering public figure of a mother with no father around, and number nineteen of twenty-one siblings, it was hard for me, to say the least. I was angry on the inside. I was hurting, but as a child I didn't quite understand why which only exacerbated my pain. Therefore, in school I was a "problem child," disruptive and misbehaving in class. Sometimes my teachers would ask me why, but I would just shrug my shoulders and say, "I don't know." I wasn't trying to be deceitful or deceptive, but I couldn't put it into words. When raised in a dysfunctional environment, dysfunctional is normal.

My teachers would get so frustrated with me while I was in middle school that they would write up a blue slip (disciplinary slip), and I would have to go to the principal's office—a visit there usually meant some type of suspension. Basically, I did little things that required me to receive in-school suspensions. Looking back at it, the school staff probably recognized that there were some issues going on in our home. Everyone in town knew that I was the nineteenth child of a twenty-one-child family, so maybe there was some mercy and consideration working on my behalf unbeknownst to me at the time. Nevertheless, I had to fulfill my in-school suspension in a big study-hall-like room. I was not allowed to interact with the kids. I usually had to stay there for two to three days before I was allowed back into my classroom. However, they had a teacher in there to monitor my behavior and to assist me with my studies.

High School

High school was quite different. In fact, it was fun even though I didn't like Horlick High School much. I attended Horlick with my siblings because we were living in an apartment complex called Douglas Terrace on Douglas Avenue. After approximately one semester at Horlick, we moved to Byrd Avenue. That put us in another school district, so I transferred to Washington Park High School.

I really enjoyed Washington Park High School even though by that time I was labeled with a learning disability that I knew I really didn't have. We experienced being teased in high school. My siblings and I were teased all the time. We didn't have a lot of nice things like other ordinary families would have. Typically, we were told that we were ugly and that we were dummies. They teased us by telling us we were always wearing the same clothes. Or they would say, "Didn't your brother have on the same clothes the other day?" Yes, that part was tough, but we managed to survive. I think that the teasing made us better people in life.

My sister Lashonda got into it with another girl. At that time, when you got into a fight with one of us, you had to fight all of us. Everybody was anticipating a big fight between Lashonda and a girl whose name I can't recall. After school in the middle of the hallway, my sister and this girl began to fight. My other sister Elsie jumped in. My nephew jumped in. My cousin jumped in. Then the girl's brother jumped in, and I jumped in, along with another one of my brothers and some of my nieces and nephews. Before you knew it, it was almost like a riot had broken out in the hallway. It had a good outcome because after that fight, no one dared mess with the Hunter family again. All the teasing and picking on us came to a screeching halt. There were no other families in the entire city that had as many brothers, sisters, and cousins as we did. Though we fought like cats and dogs among ourselves, it's still true to this day: if you fight one Hunter, you have to fight us all.

As it is for most young people, the teenage years were a time of experimentation. Like most teenagers, I did my share of experimenting. I experimented with drugs (marijuana mainly) and alcohol. Frankly, I did not like that altered-state, getting-high feeling. I remember the first time that I tried weed. I was at a party hosted by my friend Brent. I smoked, inhaled, exhaled, and never picked it up again. It just wasn't me.

One of my first experiences with alcohol occurred at a girl's house. She wanted to drink. I went out and got some beer and liquor for her because my plan was to have sex with her. I had to drink to pretend that I was with it. When you have a lot of peer pressure on you, you'll do anything. As a teenager, I just wanted to fit in, but I couldn't fit in. I wanted to fit in so badly that I was willing to do anything, and that's exactly what I did. I knew in my heart that wasn't for me because it didn't agree with my spirit. In high school I suffered from low self-esteem. I really didn't see myself as being attractive or see myself as a person that others, particularly girls, would be interested in. Therefore, I really did not have a high school sweetheart. I liked some girls and was attracted to girls, but they never gave me the time of day. In a way, a lot of girls looked at me as weird or awkward. It kind of bothered me, but at the time I was searching, trying to find myself. I was trying to be a better person.

In high school, I wore suits because I wanted to be someone important. I thought that maybe suits would attract some girls, but that didn't work either. I didn't have a high school sweetheart because I wasn't one of the jocks or one of the popular pretty boys who had all the girls hanging around them. That was fine with me. Girls just overlooked me. It could have been because of my personality, or it could have been because of my character or looks. In the long run it really didn't matter because I was too busy being me.

I enjoyed good music. During the '80s, rap music was making its debut. This was when Run DMC was out. The young people, my peers, used to love Run DMC, LL Cool J, and we also listened to Eric B and Rakim. A popular rapper during that time was Whodini, who had a song titled "Friends." There was a line in that song that really resonated with me: "Friends, how many of us have them? Friends." That song really struck a chord with me because it spoke to my circumstances; it spoke to my experience with so-called "friends."

Yes, we loved rap music back when I was in high school. Rap music was booming. People, especially the older people at that time, could not understand why young people were listening to rap. It was our own. It spoke to the heart of my generation. Others couldn't get with it, but we enjoyed rap because it was our secret language. When we listened to what artists like Run DMC or LL Cool J were saying, we felt a part of it. It was like yeah, come on. This was our thing.

There was a softer side to most of us too, so we also listened to a little bit of Luther Vandross or Patti LaBelle when we wanted to get our R&B, soul thing on. We listened to everybody, but when the rap music came on during a school assembly, we would jump up and down. We would dance and have fun because that's what we did. To this day, I enjoy rap, but now that I'm older, I see the beauty in being versatile. Not only do I listen to rap, I also listen to gospel, rock, and classical. I know some rap music is controversial. In general, however, there's nothing wrong with listening to rap because it took my generation through something, and it contributed to making us better people.

Typical High School Mischief

Like most teenagers, I had my moments of impulsivity and mischief. While attending Washington Park High School, I cut class trying to hang out with my friends. If there was a party in the middle of the day at somebody's house because their parents were out of town or it was senior skip day, I'd cut class. On one occasion, I cut a class when there was a party at a seventeen-year-old kid's house whose parents were out of town. Apparently, they left him home alone to see if he could act responsibly. A couple of friends and I skipped class and went to his house party in the middle of the day. We got there and partied down like there was no tomorrow. Several girls skipped class and came too. They were smoking weed, smoking cigarettes, drinking, the whole nine yards. Yeah, we were all being really responsible, right?

Whenever I did cut class, I didn't do it alone. After all, being mischievous wasn't any fun without others around. To me the payoff was to fit in with peers who accepted me for who I was. However, after all the fun was over, I had to hurry and get back to school before 2:45, prior to my mom arriving to pick me up. The rest of my partners in crime had to be there too because many of them rode the school bus, or their parents also picked them up. We all rushed back to the school like we had been there all day, but in reality, we had just returned.

However, even after I made it home, I still wasn't in the clear because my teachers would report my absence, and the school had a computerized system that would call the house to inform the parents, so once I got home I had to be by the phone because around six o'-clock the school computer would call and say, "Your child skipped school." I would wait by the phone or have my sisters and brothers be by the phone so they could intercept that call when it came and keep Mom from getting it because if she found out, she was going to discipline me. Between me and my siblings, we made sure we intercepted that call. When faced with having to deal with their parents' wrath, kids display a great deal of ingenuity and stealth so as not to have their mischievous deeds exposed.

Being the Preacher's Kid

Another issue that I often had to wrestle with was having a mother that was a member of the clergy. My mother considers herself to be a preacher, and I emphasize *considers*. But that being as it is, there is a lot of pressure on preachers' kids because they are caught between two realities. One reality is that they are forced to keep up appearances because of their parent's vocation. The other is they want to be normal kids, doing the normal things that kids do, fitting in with their peer group. Being caught between these two can be very difficult. The fact that you must live a moral life and always be morally upstanding is inculcated. On top of the "God don't like ugly" guilt trip that's laid on you, you also hear how you can't embarrass the minister parent. However, I guess one of the main things that always confused me was that no matter what my mother said about how people ought to act, I would often see a contradictory lifestyle behind closed doors at home.

You are told to be righteous, but when you go out into the world and see all these people doing these unrighteous *fun* things, you want to fit in with them. You know it's not right to smoke, drink, look at a dirty magazine, or have illicit sex. This seems to drive many of the preachers' kids crazy because it appears like everything fun is a sin, and that's the most important thing to teenagers, having fun with their friends.

Therefore, for me, there were a lot of conflicts resulting from being a preacher's kid because my friends would always say, "You can't go to the party tonight," especially on Saturday night, "because your family has to be at church. Your mother always has you in church." They were right. My mother did always have us in church. Most of my brothers and sisters hate church.

Back then we despised being in church, especially me. My mother considered herself to be preaching, but she couldn't preach; all she really did was scream. That's all a lot of ministers do. They don't teach or have any structured method of delivering a fulfilling sermon. All they do is scream into a microphone. Ministers like my mom scream, yell, and beat people down with the Bible. Often she used issues going on with our family as subject matter for her sermons. She rarely said anything positive. It was always something downbeat and depressing. It always left a nasty taste in my mouth.

In our family, going to church and serving God and participating in normal life activities were always played against one another. For example, everyone else could go to football games, but we were not able to because we had to go to church. We were not able to go to parties or the mall because we had to go to church.

Being a preacher's kid is a lot of pressure. One thing I noticed is that once we became adults, some of my siblings and I broke away from our mom and went to do our own thing. As a result of all this restricted living, some of us went buck-wild once we were old enough to decide for ourselves whether we wanted to participate in church. Consequently, there was a lot of rebellion and experimenting with illicit things. Sinful passions had a much greater allure because they were the things we were forbidden to do. They became things we ended up wanting to do.

We were physically, mentally, and morally (beaten up with the Bible) abused and neglected. Once some of my siblings had the chance, they started smoking, getting high on drugs, and going out to party because they had never experienced that. Some of my sisters, just like my mom, starting having children at early ages out of wedlock. By that time, all the dysfunctions were deeply imbedded. We were set up to fail by a life of forced restrictions and being made to feel as though we were different than everyone else.

The mental and the physical trauma I suffered as a child impeded my emotional development. I was an adult on the outside, but a child on the inside. My siblings were caught in youthful, impulsive, irresponsible pursuits and activities, even though they were full-grown adults. They didn't have the opportunity to do things when they were young so they ended up chasing their tails, pursuing inappropriate youthful passions and dreams from years gone by. The reality is, now that they've become old, doing those things is no longer an option.

While growing up, I enjoyed football games, and all the preaching against sports in the world could not have stopped me from liking what I liked. Sometimes my siblings and I would sneak out of the house and take off because we wanted to go to a game. One year, there was this highly anticipated football game between two schools, Park versus Horlick High. This game had been built up like the Super Bowl because there was a long-standing rivalry. I remember that my brothers and I decided we were going to that game no matter what. We didn't want to wait until Monday to hear all the stories about how great the game was.This is what we normally had to do. No, not this time. We wanted to experience it for ourselves. So, we united and said, "Forget that, I'm not going to church tonight." We chose the Friday night game over Friday night church. We went to that game and we had a good time. We didn't care about going home and getting a whipping.

There comes a point in every child's life where they get old enough to make their own decisions and choose what they want to do despite the consequences of not doing as their parents want them to do. And parents must let their children grow up. I think the Bible says that you should bring up your children in the way they shall go, so that as they get older, they will depart from it. In other words, the child may stray in life as we all do, but what's right has been instilled within them, so at some point they will return to what is right. This is why it is important to teach things like morality and the Bible in a loving, compassionate manner, not in a dictatorial way. Being a tyrant makes people rebel.

So, we went to the game and had a great time. Even though it had already been sold out and we couldn't get in, we still had a great time because we could watch the game through the fence. I do not regret it. It was great. It was fun hanging out with and socializing with other teenagers. The electrifying interaction of hundreds of young people shouting and rooting for their respective teams gave us a sense of camaraderie and togetherness. We screamed at the top of our lungs, "Let's go, Panthers!" It was exciting. It might as well have been the Super Bowl.

We were all, as it were, sitting on the edge of our seats as the two-minute warning sounded and the game was tied. That's when our team, the Panthers, had the ball and mounted a heroic drive downfield to score the winning touchdown, and we were there to see it for ourselves. There was nothing like it, and I have never forgotten that day. It made an important impression upon me. It gave me a needed sense of accomplishment, but it was also important because I had to make a choice. I needed to do what I felt was best for me versus what my mother thought was best for me. This time I chose the fun thing which also turned out to be the right thing.

CHAPTER 4

Girls: Bad Examples, the Wrong Reasons

When I considered all of the chaos and conflict that was going on around me, I knew one thing that was normal: I liked girls. By some measure I was a slow starter because my interest in the opposite sex didn't kick in until I was around sixteen years old. However, I was thrown somewhat unwittingly into my first sexual experience when I had to choose between having sex or getting beat up by my older brother Timothy. By the time I was becoming naturally attracted to girls, I was still a little bashful, particularly with the girls my age at school. I was afraid to talk to them, and I didn't know how to initiate a conversation with them. I really didn't know how to go about being in a relationship. On top of that, even though I had older brothers and sisters, I had never really been exposed to anything, but one day all that changed.

When Timothy was eighteen years old, he moved away from home and had his own apartment on Grand

Street in Racine. I was attending Washington Park High School at that time. One day after school, I stopped by Timothy's house to visit with him. However, when I knocked on the door, he didn't answer. After knocking, I checked the door, and it was unlocked, so I went in to wait for him. Finally, when he came in, he was surprised to see me and said, "You're here?"

I said, "Yeah, I'm here."

He said, "Yeah, man, I just got through having sex with this woman across the hallway. I want you to go over there and get you some too."

I said, "What do you mean, have sex with her? I'm not having sex with her."

Surprisingly, he grabbed me and said, "If you don't have sex with her, I'm going to kick your ass." So I had a no-brainer choice to make, get beat up by my brother or go over and have sex. So my brother took me over there, introduced us, and left me with her. This woman was old, in her mid-forties. To a sixteen-year-old, she might as well have been ninety. Well, as it turned out, I had sex with her, but I didn't enjoy it. It seemed nasty, so undesirable. Nevertheless, she was my first so I did it and got through, and I didn't complain about it to my brother because I didn't want to be ridiculed.

After I went back to Timothy's apartment, he was beaming and waiting to hear that I took care of business. Timothy got on the phone and called my brother Gregory and my nephew Anthony to come over. When they arrived, he announced, "Guess what you guys? Paul had sex for the first time." To my surprise, it turned out to be a celebratory event. It was like a big old party.

Gregory asked me, "So, how did you like it?"

I told Gregory, "Don't say anything, but I didn't like it at all. I don't want to do it again. It hurt real bad."

My brother replied, "It did?"

I said, "Yeah. I don't know what happened, but I started feeling real strange, and all of a sudden this white gooey stuff shot out my penis. It was a feeling that I never felt before. I don't want to have sex anymore."

Gregory, kind of perplexed, replied, "Aah, okay."

However, Timothy was sounding the trumpet like I had just climbed Mount Everest. He felt like it was the greatest thing I had ever done in my life because he was really into having sex himself. He told everyone about it. "Yeah, I got my baby brother laid." After a while, he started calling me to come over. At that time, I didn't know what he was doing. Unfortunately, I was being groomed to be "a player." He used to tell me, "Don't be faithful to a woman. Always have multiple women." That's how I was mentored when it came to relationships with females, and I picked up this so-called player's mantle from my brother. I lived by the code: don't develop meaningful relationships with women. Be unfaithful to them. Be dishonest with them. To my surprise, Timothy wasn't the only one who thought that way, but several other men lived by the same rules. As a result, I was having sexual relationships with women that I actually didn't care for beyond the sex, nothing serious.

By the time I turned eighteen, I began to call myself a player because my brother taught me how to rap (smooth-talk the girls) to win them over. He used to tell me to always tell them how pretty they were and how much I needed them, and how I had to have them. Soon I had a practiced silver tongue because my brother had instructed me on how to win a girl's heart with the right words. However, he always cautioned me not to fall for them or get too attached. "That's being weak," he insisted. "Don't settle down with one woman. Always have someone else on the side. That's how real men handle it. Real men have multiple women."

So, as a typical young man who had no good examples of how to be a good man, all I wanted from women was sex, no relationship whatsoever. I didn't care about women crying or being emotional. I just wanted sex. I wouldn't have a conversation with them. I wouldn't listen to them or be concerned about what was going on in their lives. I didn't want the person. I just wanted the goodies.

Now that I'm older, I realize that real men have wives. Real men are looking for companionship and respect others' feelings. Real men love the Lord. Real men seek after God. Real men chase God. Real men pray every day. Real men are in touch with their feelings and never set out to abuse anyone else. Real men are leaders and set good examples for their children and other youth. Real men are responsible and act responsibly. Real men can handle the truth and seek the truth. Real men aren't afraid to say, "God, I need you." That's what real men do. Real men don't pursue women to abuse them, but real men pursue God to be better men.

As a historic footnote, this mind-set that my brother taught me about women has plagued the African-American community. Irresponsible men contributed to the breakdown of the family unit. The skewed philosophy that woman are just a piece of meat to use and abuse has almost ruined our people. It can be traced back to a slave mentality, where black men were studded just like horses and cattle. They were used for procreation, to produce more slaves. They were not allowed to be in any relationship with the slave women that they impregnated. In order to please their masters, they did their job well and were praised for doing a good job—impregnating women. If one had to choose between backbreaking forced labor from sun up to sun down or having a job as a baby-maker, most would choose the latter. Hundreds of years of this kind of conditioning caused this type of mind-set to be deeply rooted in many black men, where it was seen as an honor to go around making babies that you don't take care of or support. As a matter of fact, you were applauded and told, "That's being a man."

However, there is much more to simply siring a child. You need only be a male to do that—that's not being a man. Being a man is taking on the responsibility of raising and fathering the children you bring into this world. Whether you're married or not, it's still your responsibility.

Unfortunately, that mind-set has hindered my relationship with the mother of my children. That's too bad. Now that I'm out of that relationship, I'm not seeking a woman. I'm seeking to be a better person, a better man. I want to be a real man that will seek God, praise God, pray, pursue after God's own heart. That's what I want to be. I ended just wanting to have sex. It's not even worth it. One thing I learned about sex is that you are going to have your peaks, and you are going to have your valleys. I learned that it's not about sex. It's about having a relationship with God and developing meaningful relationships with other people.

Everywhere you look you see sensuality and sex. As they say, sex sells. Many Hollywood executives won't produce a movie unless it has some sex. You can't watch a commercial on the television unless there are sexual overtones. Everything seems to be about being sexy or having sex appeal. Television commercials sell everything from breakfast cereal to male sexual enhancement products with sexual innuendo, inundating the airwaves with messages that sex is the most important thing to be pursued. It's really ridiculous.

However, my mind is not on sex anymore. My mind is on much more important things. I take this opportunity to say to the women reading this book who I engaged with sexually, I want to offer my sincere apology for mistreating you. I was being selfish and immature. I hope that you can find it within yourselves to forgive me.

I wish that some man would have become a mentor to me when I was a teenager and showed me the right road to take. I wish some man had showed me that it's not your libido or length that determines the measure of a man. I wish someone had been there to say, "Young man, it's about having a relationship with God and having respect for yourself and others. That's what's important, not these five-minute thrills that bring a lifetime of consequences and pain." I wish someone had told me, "It's not about being a player which is really being a fool and degrading yourself. A decent man is faithful to one woman, and that's what any decent woman expects from a man." Unfortunately, no one was there to be a good role model for me or my brothers and sisters. No one was there to correct us, to discipline us or say, "No, that is wrong." I missed having a father.

If someone had been there for my siblings and me when my brother passed away and when my father passed away, we would have been better kids. I wish someone had been there to teach us about relationships, substance abuse, and how to respect one another. I ended up being a grown man with a teenager's mentality. I really needed someone when I was a teenager. I was lost. I was a renegade. I didn't care. But looking back on it, I needed a father figure.

I wish my dad was alive. But he's gone, and I had to learn from my failures and mistakes. Though I can't undo the past, I do have the power to make the right decisions today and move forward from here. Those of you reading this book who knew me when I was messed up and confused, know that today my eyes and ears are opened and my heart is new. With God's divine help, I am a better man today, and I shall make it to my destiny, and become the man that God has called me to be.

CHAPTER 5
Love and Charity
Mission Impossible

One of the problems with my mother is she has the need to feel important. She wants to be the one in charge. Oddly, her need to be dominant is really based in deep-rooted low self-esteem. You see, my mother does not function well being under other people. That's when all of her inadequacies and inabilities are revealed. She avoids any situation where her shortcomings become evident. Therefore, she is driven by a need to be in charge.

E is also driven by having people look up to her. She wants people to look up to her and to revere her, but this is where the great conflict comes in: my mother doesn't deserve to be a leader because she's a hypocrite. She wants to be recognized. She wants her face in the paper; furthermore, she wants to be on television. She wants the world to read about how fantastic she is as she goes out to save the world. That's how she is portrayed in her book, *Love and Charity*. Unfortunately, that book is full of half-truths. The real story has not been told. My mother wants people to know an idealized

Louise Hunter that has never really existed.

I believe my mother went into social services as an extension of her ego. It was not some altruistic or divine calling. It was about fulfilling a need to cover her low self-esteem with good works and accomplishments. Therefore, what looked like a great benevolent and humanitarian effort was really a veneer for her self-serving purposes. On that basis, my mother started up her charitable outreaches and shelters and began building an empire where she, and she alone, would be an uncontested queen. I must admit that for decades, despite criticism, adversity, and tragedy, she pulled it off. She should never have started a shelter

A couple of years after my dad passed away, my mom decided to start a shelter. She did it from our home. I was a little boy, too young to understand why my mother was having all these strange people living with us. I remember having mixed emotions about the whole thing. I remember those first few indigent men she took in at our house on State Street in Racine. To put this in the right perspective, we had a very large family, and we were barely making it on our own. Nevertheless, my mother started taking in homeless people.

Now on the surface that sounds so benevolent, but in reality it was very foolish on her part. There was no man of the house anymore, other than my older brothers who, of course, were in and out of the house. The homeless are usually homeless for a reason. All too often the reasons are bad ones like drug addiction, mental illness, or felonies such as child molestation. My mother was not sophisticated when it came to screening many of these characters. She had no professional training whatsoever although she did become better at this as the years went by.

My mother always claimed that God told her to start a homeless shelter, but she didn't start out with the mission that she has today. At first it was a small outreach called the Love and Charity Club. By the time

I was born, she had moved the outreach out of our house. In the home operation she was known around the community for baking cookies for school kids and making food baskets out of donated food for the needy, but it wasn't a homeless shelter yet. The homeless shelter came only after my father died.

To be honest with you, I believe in my heart that God never called E to be the leader of Love and Charity. She said that God called her, but that's subjective. I believe the reality is, if God calls you to do something, He will also equip you to do the work. He's going to give you the resources. He will instruct you on what you need to do. He will lead you to the right path, even if it means returning to school to perfect the natural gifts that He has already put in you. You may be naturally gifted to teach, but if you do not go back to school and get an education to perfect and enhance that natural gift, you will never teach in school or a university. Some things are not possible without the proper credentials.

Regardless of no education, no credentials, no management skills, no fiduciary skills, my mother started the mission anyway. Looking back at everything now, she shouldn't have ever started. The reason I say this is because she never really knew how to manage the operation itself or manage the people she solicited to help run the shelter. Ironically, my mom loved calling in educated people, but she would never listen to them. What she really wanted was a bunch of "yes" men and women to surround her, who would agree with her bad decisions and ill-advised ventures.

E always claimed she was trained by the best, and whenever I asked her who that was, she always said Mother Alexander trained her. In *Love and Charity*, there is a chapter titled "Image of a Godly Woman." In that chapter, my mother talks about being influenced by a woman named Mother Alexander. When you read that account, you would think that my mother laid at this woman's feet hanging on her every word and learning all she could about how to be a real humanitarian. Although that all sounds good and makes good reading in her biography, the fact is it wasn't quite that way.

When you asked other people who knew Mother Alexander, they would tell you that she never encouraged my mother to start a homeless shelter, nor did she train my mother on how to run a mission. The word around town was that my mother has always been very difficult to deal with. She never wanted to sit under anyone to be taught. She never wanted to be under anyone's leadership. She never wanted to be accountable to anyone. She always wanted to be the captain of her own ship and determine her own course without any rebuttal from anyone.

My mother never wanted to sit still. She always would jump and shout and show the world how spiritual she was, but she wouldn't sit still for anyone to instruct her on the proper way to do things. With those mechanisms working in her, no wonder she became so hard to deal with. No one was able to work with my mom for any length of time. No matter who it was, they started out really gung-ho with lots of drive, but sooner or later, E's other side would kick in and she would destroy that relationship. Whenever someone new would come around the mission to help out, we would all wonder, "How long is this one going to last?"

Yes, my mother said that she loved to help people, but strangely, in my mother's mind, love was a weapon. Love was not healing and helping. Love was a stick to hit you over the head with. For Louise Hunter this seemed to be the greatest contradiction of all. As she touted the ideas of love thy neighbor and give assistance to the poor and needy, she found it much easier to express those actions outside the confines of her own home towards strangers than toward her very own brood. Even though my mother carried the title Christian, she rarely actually lived the life of a true one.

Sure, she would run and say Jesus, Jesus, Jesus,

and offer up fervent prayers, but it was all done hypo-critically. My mother played the game, and all my sib-lings came up watching her play the game. Many of them played the game too while others got out of the game altogether, having nothing to do with God or the church.

My mother has had great difficulty expressing love to anyone, especially us. For example, she never says she loves us. That's right, my mother has never gen-uinely told me that she loves me. When she does say it, it's merely perfunctory and fake—there's no heart in it at all. She rarely is maternally affectionate. She doesn't give any of us a big mother's loving, embracing hug. She's never held us as any loving mother would and should. We have always felt that we were an embarrass-ment to our mom. We were very useful whenever the media or the cameras were around, whenever we were all required to smile for the camera like in the *Ebony* pic-ture. That's when E wanted us around to show the world that "the lady with all those kids" is really a success story.

After the media was gone, my mother didn't even want to be seen in public with us, not even to have din-ner with her own children in public.

The Mission Used to Be a Great Place!

Before I go any further, let me be clear. There was a time that the mission was in its heyday. During much of the 1980s, Love and Charity was at its prime. Back then, it was very professional because there were edu-cated and professional individuals on her Board of Di-rectors. At one time, there were executives from local corporations, millionaires, entrepreneurs, community activists and concerned citizens that all brought a level of expertise and prestige to Love and Charity. At one point the mayor of Racine was on the Board of Directors. My mother had a pastor of an influential church and college professors. Just about everyone wanted to be involved with Mother Hunter's Love and Charity Mission. I mean, who could resist the story of how we were about to become homeless ourselves, and someone gave us an eighteen-room house for the price of one dollar? I mean, that story still brings tears to my eyes.

Back during those years, my mother received all kinds of recognition. She received the prestigious Jefferson Award. She also received commendations from the State Senator, the Governor, the City of Racine, the Police Department, Sheriff's Department, on and on. She collected thousands upon thousands of dollars in in-kind donations, as well as money that practically flooded into Love and Charity.

On holidays like Thanksgiving and Christmas, food lines would stretch around the block, where the needy could get a warm meal or take home enough food to feed a family for a week. Even outside the mission, my mother would put out tables of bread and other pastries that people could walk up and take. News media from Racine and Milwaukee would always come down to cover what Love and Charity was doing for the community. It was great. Most of my brothers and sisters who were around during those years all enjoyed Mom's and Love and Charity's celebrity too.

There was one memorable event where my mother was honored by the citizens of Racine called Share Your Prayers. It seemed like all of the who's who of Racine, Milwaukee, Kenosha and other surrounding towns came out to honor my mother. There was even a young lady who was legally blind that my mother had prayed for. Amazingly the blind lady received a remarkable portion of her sight back. When this woman gave her testimony, the whole place went up in thunderous applause for my mother. There were definitely some positives in my mother's career as an advocate for the disenfranchised. However, the problem was that the public got all the good stuff. The strangers got all the "love and charity," but not the Hunter children. This is where the whole irony of the matter lies.

After the heyday years had gone by, the mission started to decline. It wasn't because the donations weren't coming or because there were no people to service. That wasn't the case at all. As the years went by, my mother's leadership became increasingly erratic and her board members started bailing one by one. When that began to happen, things started to deteriorate. Love and Charity's board members used to make informed recommendations to her about what the shelter could do as far as offering a wider array of services to the community and telling her about funding options that not-for-profits could apply for, but no matter how sound their advice and counsel was, my mother would reject, object, and oppose any idea that was not hers. Eventually, argumentative board meetings resulted, where it was either E's way or the highway, and the board members quickly became fed up and resigned.

One of the key issues that used to give my mother a lot of anxiety was when the board used to make recommendations of getting federal, state, and local grants for funding. My mother was dead set against receiving grants from the government, unwilling to believe that was the way to go as far as funding was concerned. She only wanted donations from the community, like businesses and from individuals. The main reason why I believe she was so dead set against government funding was she did not want to be accountable to some higher authority, especially the government. She didn't want anyone looking over her shoulder.

When applying for grants, you have to agree to stick to your budget and only spend as line items dictate. With grants there is accountability, audits, and oversight, none of which my mother wanted. My mother wanted to hold both the purse and the purse strings, with no one to answer to when it came to the mission's finances. So, whenever someone came to the mission with a financial donation, she would take the money and spend it as she pleased and not keep accurate records of all transactions. Granted, the money was usually spent on things relating to the mission, but she did have the freedom to do what she wanted with the funds. In reality, my mother treated Love and Charity as if it were a sole proprietorship, where she basically did what she wanted to. The only problem with that is that Love and Charity is a federally tax-exempt charitable corporation that no one person owns.

Another real issue with keeping the government out was that my mother wanted to conduct religious services in the mission. Therefore, she felt that she couldn't do so and get state or federal funding. Though there is some truth to that, it's only partly true. The fact is, had she let the professionals on the board do their job, she could have had programming to service both secular and religious functions. She could have had an operating budget that was state or federally funded, but under those funding guidelines, she couldn't force her residents to attend services. And that's what she wanted to do, make it mandatory to attend religious services where she was preacher.

She threatened the very people that came to the mission for help, the people that looked up to her and called her "Mother Hunter." When this type of behavior got back to the Board of Directors, it also caused them to resign.

To overcome all of the defections of her board members, my mother quickly came up with the idea to start filling those vacancies with people who were staying at the mission. This by itself was a conflict of interest and strategic mistake at many levels. The very people who obviously could not manage their own lives now found themselves on the Board of Directors of a not-for-profit organization that reaped thousands of dollars of donations and revenues annually. As a reward, my mother took the opportunity to dictate whatever policy or rule she wanted, with absolutely no chance of resistance from her Board of Directors that depended on Love and Charity for their food and shelter.

CHAPTER 6

A Mother's Two Faces

"If I speak in the tongues of men or of angels, but do not have love, I am only a resounding gong or a clanging cymbal.[2] If I have the gift of prophecy and can fathom all mysteries and all knowledge, and if I have a faith that can move mountains, but do not have love, I am nothing.[3] If I give all I possess to the poor and give over my body to hardship that I may boast, but do not have love, I gain nothing.[4] Love is patient, love is kind. It does not envy, it does not boast, it is not proud.[5] It does not dishonor others, it is not self-seeking, it is not easily angered, it keeps no record of wrongs.[6] Love does not delight in evil but rejoices with the truth.[7] It always protects, always trusts, always hopes, always perseveres." 1 Cor. 13:1-7

Back in ancient Greece, history records a society

that was in love with being entertained. The ancient Greeks were known for their sports events, games, and their theater. In their plays, there would often be characters that acted behind a mask. Unlike today's actors, who in most cases are shown as themselves but are portraying someone else—the ancient Greek actor often hid behind a mask. Therefore, the audience saw only the mask as the actor portrayed that character, but underneath was the real person. The Greeks had a name for this duality called *hypokrites*, where our English word *hypocrite* comes from. As defined by the *Merriam-Webster's Collegiate Dictionary*, a hypocrite is: "a person who puts on a false appearance of virtue or religion."

As portrayed by the ancient Greek actors, the mask allowed them to act as one person, who the audience would see, when in fact they were really someone else. Such was the case when it came to my mother; she had two faces: one real, the other one not. One face, her public face, was this positive, loving, caring, benevolent, larger-than-life character, whose sole mission was to save and rescue all the lost and dejected disenfranchised unfortunates of the world. The other face, the one that was negative, critical, insensitive, self-centered, and self-serving, only came out behind closed doors when all the cameras and the lights were gone, and the mask was taken away.

While we were growing up, my mom would always be negative, putting down my sisters and brothers, my nieces and nephews, my aunts, cousins, and other relatives. As children, we loved going to visit my dad's relatives. We could play and visit with family members from my dad's side. My mother always discouraged us from wanting to be a part of their lives because she would say, "They never did like us." As a result of her negative words being drilled into us, we rarely spoke to them. We had been turned against them. We would just say hi and bye. We never had a long, extended conversation. That's the way our mother kept us from exploring anything outside our own little world that she had created at Love and Charity. As I would learn later on in life, all those negative seeds were used to control us, to keep us from being freed from the treachery of her bondage, in a prison of low-self esteem, despondency, and dependence.

The only thing I can say when it comes to my mom is that there is a great conflict within her. Though indeed there are two distinct faces, there is only one person, and as she has grown older, she has less wherewithal to compartmentalize the two faces, for now the dark side has mostly taken over. Now she rarely says anything positive. The glass is always half empty, never half full. She despises those who are doing well, particularly if they ever had anything to do with the mission. One minute, she just loves you. The next minute, she hates your guts. As a child, I couldn't understand what was wrong with her. One minute she was building you up; the next minute she was tearing you down. I always wondered what was going on with her. She had two personalities, and because of those two personalities, it was hard dealing with her because you were never sure which person you were going to get.

My mother's two faces were further evidenced in the fact that she had all these children, twenty-one in all, eighteen living, but she really didn't love any of us. True love is evidenced in the passage of Scripture that I quoted at the being of this chapter. According to this definition of love, my mother never truly loved any of her own children. This is proven by her actions of callous indifference and at times downright cold hardness. The question that has always remained in the hearts of my brothers and sisters is, "Where is the love?"

As benevolent as she appears to the world, she has no real love for others. She loves superficially, through the veneer of good works, but only as long as the good works benefit her. How could I say this? How could this be? One would ask or should I say challenge me and say, "Hasn't your mother shown how much she loves by the things that she has done? Hasn't she helped thousands of people over the years? Hasn't she done what the Bible says and fed the hungry, clothed the naked, comforted the downtrodden? Hasn't she done all these things and been recognized for her numerous accomplishments?" The answer to all these questions is both yes and no. Both answers are appropriate because she has two different faces, but she has only one heart, and that heart at the very core is bitter, angry, and hurting.

The Bible also says, "Love thy neighbor as thyself." This of course assumes that you first love your own self. My mother cannot truly love others because I really believe she does not love herself. I think my mother experienced some very traumatic times growing up because she tries to conceal her past. She never wants to talk about it. There is nothing wrong with acknowledging your mistakes and sharing your past with people because if you have learned, others can learn from your failures.

But, the two faces of my mother are very hard to understand. One minute she would say something positive, and those positive things that she would say would always be about Jesus. But the majority of the time—I would say ninety-nine percent of the time—she would be saying something negative, always the two faces.

One face that you didn't want to see was the negative side. She would lie about you. She would try to destroy you. She would contradict you. She would say you don't know what you're talking about—you never have and you never will. She would say to you, "I know more than you because I was born before you and I'm older than you." Those are the things that she used to say to my siblings.

Just in case those of you reading this book think that I am being overly critical of my mother, not too long ago there was a big lie she told that got many of my family members in a big uproar. My own mother lied and told as many family members as she could persuade that I and the author of my mom's biography, Dennis Woods, stole over a million dollars from the sales of that book from her. First of all, Dennis is the author of that book, not my mother. The book is *about* her, but it's not *her* book.

I stated earlier that at one time during the early 1990s, Dennis lived at Love and Charity, but today he is an entrepreneur that owns a few different businesses. His story is literally a rags-to-riches story. Dennis and his wife live in a large, beautiful home in a suburb of Chicago. One day Dennis invited my mom and me up to his house, and when we arrived, my mother was floored. To tell you the truth, so was I. The house is a small mansion, beautiful and elegantly furnished. I was actually glad to see that someone who used to live at Love and Charity was doing so well. It really made me proud, and I thought my mother would have the same sentiments, but behind closed doors, she didn't.

After we left, my mother started saying some unbelievable things about Dennis. Jealously, she began saying, "Ain't no Christian supposed to live like that. He's got to be doing something wrong!" I couldn't believe my ears. She wasn't happy for him at all. She only pretended to be when she was there. Several months after that, we had to stop at Dennis' house to pick up some *Love and Charity* books because my mother was doing a speaking engagement in Springfield, Illinois. We had driven over two hours to get there, and when we pulled up, my mother refused to even get out of the car. She wouldn't allow those who accompanied us on the trip to get out. I was told to go into Dennis' house for the books, and she insisted that I hurry up.

We still had about a three-hour drive to Springfield, but she wouldn't allow people to get out to stretch their legs, get some water, or even use the bathroom. By this time she had talked so evilly about Dennis to everyone that letting them go into his house would have contradicted everything she had been saying about a man who was obviously blessed. When we pulled up, the lady that was driving began saying, "This is a beautiful house. I love his landscaping." When we pulled away, my mom started up again, with her jealousy, hatred, and lies. "He got that house off of the million dollars that he stole from me." I just shook my head and held my peace.

This is just one example of how my mom really ticks. At her core, she hates Dennis because of his success. She's not happy for him at all. When he was living at the mission back in the 90s, she dogged him out, but like most "thinking" people, he had a mind of his own and left the mission to move on to bigger and better things.

The night before he left the mission, my mother stretched forth her hand at him and prophesied, "Young man, in thirty days, you'll be looking for a place to eat, and wish you were back here at Love and Charity." Well, as you can see, that was a false prophecy. Sadly, the day Dennis left the mission, all he had to his name was a garment bag and a green military duffle bag filled with all his worldly possessions. A mission resident by the name of Larry Schafer, my mother's assistant, was going to give Dennis a ride to the bus station in the mission truck, but when my mother heard that, she came outside and refused to let Larry take Dennis to the bus station. She was going to make him walk there. However, my older brother Larry was there, and he gave Dennis a ride to the bus station. Imagine it, after all of that, Dennis still wrote my mother's book and made her look like a queen.

The Bible says, "You shall know them by their fruit." The fruit that my mother bears makes it obvious to whose kingdom she really belongs. Though she has all the outward trappings of a Christian, she's not part of God's kingdom; she's a part of the devil's kingdom.

The other day, I was listening to a preacher. In his sermon, he said that sometimes you can be fired by God and don't even know that you have been fired. He said that God is the only boss that will fire you and allow you to keep working. What he means is that God will remove the anointing from your life without you knowing it. In other words, you can still preach and teach and cause people to come to the Lord, but you yourself can be a castaway. This is how it is with my mom—the anointing has been removed, and she, for quite some time now, has already been fired.

My mom has done many corrupt things to people, particularly those who stayed at Love and Charity. I've seen it personally. Love and Charity is her god. Anyone who messes with her god, and she will try to destroy them. She will lie about them. She will tell her kids, "This is what happened. This man tried to jump on me. This man hit me." Some of my brothers and sisters will go off on some of the residents of Love and Charity. What my mother would often do is say derogatory things to the residents at the mission. She would beat them up mentally and push their buttons to a point where someone would go off on her. Then, she could say, "He's trying to hit me. Call the police." That's what she wanted to do. Call the police. Sometimes she would be successful in her disruptive, evil little plans. The police would come and escort a resident out, but most of the time the police wouldn't get involved.

I can recall one summer when the mission truck was broken down and needed a starter. There was an individual who knew how to fix it, and he got word that Louise Hunter wanted him to come to the mission to repair the truck. When he arrived there, he was outside and he stuck his head in the door and said to my mom he couldn't come in because he was smoking a cigarette, but once he got through he would come in. After finishing his cigarette, he decided to come in.

When he came in, my mother totally went off on

this young man. She said to him, "What you doin' without no shirt? Who told you to come down here?"

He said, "Well, I got word that you wanted me to come down and fix the truck. You wanted me to put the starter on the truck."

She said, "Yeah, I want you to put the starter on the truck. But listen here, once you put the starter on the truck, I don't want you to go and buy no dope. That's all you want to do is do dope and get high. That's what you're going to do with the money."

I was sitting in the kitchen eating breakfast at this time. The man looked my mother in the eye and said, "Fuck you, bitch," and he turned around and walked out of the shelter.

When he did that, I just looked at my mom, and she said to me, "Are you going to go and beat him up? You heard what he said."

I said to my mom, "You should have never said what you said to provoke this man. He was coming over to help you save money by fixing the truck for half price. You should have never said those words to that young man because whatever he does with what he gets paid is his business."

The man walked out of the shelter and started to walk up Douglas Avenue. Within minutes my two nephews pulled up. Once they arrived, my mother went on ranting, telling them what had happened. My two nephews ran after the guy. When they caught up to him, he was getting into a car with a friend. They wanted to jump on him. When they got close to the car and told the guy what they were going to do, the guy pulled out a gun and said, "What do you want to do?" They backed off and came back to the shelter.

I explained to them what had happened, and they were very upset that my mother almost got them killed. My mother would never be truthful and honest with anyone. It's just not in her to be truthful. E could have gotten both of my nephews killed by intentionally manipulating them. By being a deceiver and an instigator, she almost caused them to lose their lives. If they had died, my mother would not have had any compassion. She would have never told the truth about what really led up to a tragic incident that didn't have to happen. That's the evil side of her two faces.

I've seen this evil woman at work. I have seen this woman destroy residents' lives at Love and Charity. This woman is wicked. This woman is evil. This woman is sneaky. She will backstab you. She does not have compassion for people. Sometimes I wonder how she could say God called her with the things that she does to try to destroy peoples' lives.

My mother's coldhearted ways are known to all of my siblings. We have all experienced hell dealing with this woman. Just imagine having a relationship with her. You can't sit down and have a conversation with her without being on guard because you never know which face she will be wearing. All of us have always longed for our mother's true love and affection. So, whenever she puts on the loving face, we are all susceptible to falling for it, but only because we ache for our mother's love and acceptance, just like any other child would. However, we all have enough experience with E to know, don't get too comfortable with her loving happy face because that face baits you to be drawn in closer. Once you are in too close, there comes the evil face, the face that destroys, the face that tears you down, the face that dogs you, the face that hurts your feelings, the face that is self-centered and self serving, that dastardly evil face.

There was another incident I witnessed when I was at Love and Charity. My brother Gregory and I were having a conversation in the kitchen. He was telling me that he was about to check himself in for rehab because he was using drugs. He was hooked on crack. I felt his pain. He began to share with me that he had been doing crack cocaine and that he no longer could control it. He stated that he really needed to get some help. There were some residents around, and my mother was listening to the conversation that we were having. She never said to Gregory, "I'll help you son. I'll call the hospital or the rehab center to get you some professional help. Whatever it takes, if you are willing to kick those drugs, I'll support you and love you through this thing until you are free." She said nothing of the sort.

She walked up, got between my brother and me, and said to me, "Paul, have you ever thought about using drugs?"

I said to her, "No."

She said again, "You never thought about trying it?"

I said, "No. I don't want to do drugs. That's not for me."

My brother Gregory said, "E, Paul does not hang around the people that I do. He doesn't hang around people who smoke drugs."

Then she said, "Oh, I just thought maybe he wanted to do it."

At that point I looked at my brother and said, "Let's go downstairs and talk." As we went downstairs, I said, "She wants me on drugs, but she will never see that day because my mind is not on drugs. My mind is on trying to make it in this world, trying to be successful in this world, trying to graduate from college." When we got downstairs, I told my brother, "Hey, you know what you have to do, so go do it. You take care of it. You move on with your life." I told him, "I love you, and the only thing I can do is pray for you."

Another incident occurred in 2011 while I was enrolled in college. My mother had a Mercedes, two vans, and another car. I wanted to use the van to go to school. However, she wouldn't let me use the van. At the time, I was unemployed, living on sixty-one dollars a week in unemployment. I used to take that van and drive it to school, but my mother didn't want me using the van;

she wanted me to buy it. I told her, "I don't have any money to buy the van. I'm living off of sixty-one dollars a week in unemployment, and I'm living inside this shelter. You think I can afford it?"

Do you think she cared? No, she didn't care. She ended up telling my sister Zollena as well as some of my other siblings, "I am going to sell that van. I'm not giving it to him." (The van was worth at least twelve to fifteen-hundred dollars.) She said, "I am going to sell it, and I don't care if I only get a couple hundred dollars for it. I refuse to give it to Paul because I don't want to see that nigger succeed in life."

She sold it, but before she sold it, she told my sister Zollena, "I want to see that nigger walk. I don't want to see that nigger drive a car or nothing. I want to see that nigger walk. That's what I want to do. I want to see him walk. I want to see him suffer."

Can you imagine words like those coming from your own mother? If I was a weak person, words like those would have long destroyed me. It happened with several of my brothers and sisters. Because of my mother, we are a completely dysfunctional family. However, those of us who were able to stay strong and move on in life are doing well. The others sank deeper into dysfunction. Nevertheless, in one way or another, we were all victims of a cruel, venomous mother.

So, what ended up happening was she sold that fifteen-hundred-dollar van for three hundred dollars, and I walked. E was pleased with that. She was happy with that because she did not want to see me succeed in life. She bragged to the residents who lived in the mission, "Yeah, I sold it 'cause I don't want to see him drive. I want to see that nigger walk. I don't want to see him have anything in life."

Little did she know or have the decency to understand that not having a vehicle would not keep me from reaching my goal of graduating from college. Through the cold and snow, I walked to school. I was able to walk because for a full year my classes were in Racine. If my classes were in Milwaukee, I would have gotten a ride from Jasmine Lohr. I walked to school in inclement, blustery, winter weather, determined to make it anyhow. During the summer months it was easier because I could ride my bike. One pedal at a time, I got closer to my goal, and I kept saying over in my mind, "You cannot stop me." I had made up my mind that I was going to persevere, no matter what, even if it meant overcoming the two faces of E.

Here's yet another example to show you the two sides of Mrs. Hunter. I remember being at the shelter and coming downstairs because I needed to get to the bank so I could send my kids some money in San Antonio, Texas. My niece Jaqueetta was there, and I asked her to take me to the bank. She said to me, "Well, Uncle Paul, I really can't take you right now, but you can use my car to go to the bank."

I said, "Okay."

When I said that, my mother looked at Jaqueetta in that evil way and stared at her. My niece gave me the key. I went to her car, drove it to the bank, and after leaving the bank, I sent the money to my daughter. When I got back to the shelter, my mother was in her office. My niece said, "Do you know what grandma said?"

I asked, "What?"

"She told me that you don't have any driver's license. Soon as you left, she said, 'Girl, I don't know why you let Paul drive your car. He doesn't have any driver's license whatsoever. Why did you let him drive your car?' I told her that I didn't know that you didn't have a driver's license. She said, 'Yeah, he don't have no license. That's the reason why I don't let him drive the mission vehicle because he doesn't have any license.'"

I told my niece, "You know what? I do have a driver's license." Every time that Zollena (my older sister) let me use her vehicle, E would tell her the same lie too.

That's what I'm talking about, one face smiles at you, and the other will lie about you and to you.

One might ask, "Well why didn't you guys confront your mother about all of these things?" However, whenever anyone confronted my mom on these issues, she would lie and say, "Hey, I didn't say that. What are you talking about? I did not even say that to that girl. That girl is lying. I did not say that to her." That's what my mom would say.

The positive and negative faces will fight each other. Like the Bible says, you cannot serve two masters. You will either love one or hate the other. She loves that negative side. She really does. Sometimes I just sit back and look at her and analyze her because with her it's all about being negative.

My mother doesn't function in an environment where everything is going well. That's not her environment of choice. Her environment of choice is chaos, disruption, controversy, contention, and conflict. When these things are occurring, my mother thrives because then there is a mess to manage, and she can come out smelling like a rose, looking like a hero, looking like an angel of light.

Every morning since I've been living at the mission, I get up about seven-thirty and I meditate for half an hour. By eight-thirty I'm coming downstairs, and she always has all the guys gathered for a meeting. She always wants to be the center of attention, so in the morning when I come down there, they are in the kitchen. It's just like that old slave mentality, where you just keep whipping on them and whipping on them. That's what she does. Since I have been living here, I have never seen her cancel a meeting. Those meetings take place every morning, and she always has something negative to say.

One of my goals in life is to be positive in every possible opportunity. Having a positive attitude gives me the motivation to succeed in realizing my goals. When I get up in the morning, I don't want to hear anything negative. I want to hear people say something positive like "Jesus is alive."

Like I said, that particular morning I was just ready to go. I got up. She was in a meeting with the residents, and she was hammering them. She was talking about how they were drinking, selling her meat, and stealing from the shelter. She said to me, "What do you think?"

I said to her, "I just got through praying and meditating. When I come downstairs, I want something positive deposited into my life. I don't want to hear anything negative." I told her to keep her negative comments to herself. She did not like what I said, but that was the truth. I just told her straight out, "I don't want to hear anything negative. I want to hear something positive." I wanted some words of encouragement to be deposited into my life so I could go on that particular day, encouraged, energized, ready to go.

She got very upset. I didn't say a word. I grabbed my book bag, looked at her and smiled, and I just rode my bike to my next destination.

Like I say, you don't want to meet those two faces. It's evil. It's wicked. This woman is filled with dismay. Sometimes I think she has Alzheimer's, dementia. She is always forgetting things. She will put something down. Then, she can't find it, and she'll accuse someone of taking it.

Another time at Love and Charity, one of the residents there was accused of smoking pot. My mother was in Memphis, Tennessee. She called the guy and said to him, "The Lord is telling me that you smoking weed in my shelter."

The guy said, "No, I'm not smoking weed."

"Well, somebody called and told me that you were smoking weed."

The man said, "I'm not smoking weed in your shelter, Mrs. Hunter. Your son has been here. Your daughter has been here. I have not been smoking weed."

"Well, you have been smoking weed in my shelter. That's what the Lord said, and that's what somebody told me."

My mom just totally started to beat this guy up. "You know you're smoking weed. You know you're doing it."

This was the conversation over the phone between the two. The man sat there and just cried. He told my mother, "I'm not smoking weed in your shelter. Mrs. Hunter, I would not do that." He just sat there and cried and cried.

Two days later, my mom got back from Memphis, and she was still on him about that. "You were smoking weed in my shelter. You just been smoking weed. You a liar and you going to hell. You call yourself a Christian? You going to hell. God gonna punish you for lying to me, and I'm an old woman." She always used that line, "I'm an old woman. You lying to this old woman."

The man said, "Mrs. Hunter, I was not smoking inside your shelter. I wasn't smoking cigarettes. I wasn't smoking weed. I wasn't doing anything illegal in your shelter." He cried like a little baby because he was being honest with my mom.

We found some weed inside the shelter, and she thought it was his. Somebody was smoking weed in the shelter, and that person came forth. It was my sister! She was smoking weed inside the shelter. When my sister came forth to confess that she was the one that was smoking weed on the women's and the men's side of the shelter, and she left it on the men's side, my mother couldn't believe it. She said, "You're lying. You're lying because you want my man," referring to the resident. "You want my man. That's why you're saying you did it because you want my man." That's the way she referred to the residents at Love and Charity. Those are her men. Those are her people—what insanity!

But my sister told my mother on several occasions, "I was the one. I take full responsibility for it. You don't have to put him out. I was the one that was smoking weed."

Then my mother started to hammer her and beat her up. "Your daddy said y'all would never be anything. That's what your daddy used to say. Now you're the one smoking weed in my shelter? Your daddy said you would never be nothing. He said it. He said, 'These kids are going to give me a hard time. These kids will never be nothing, never amount to anything.'" She started to constantly beat up on my sister with negative statements. It was just like shooting a machine gun—all the bullets come out. When you are dealing with Louise Hunter, she shoots those bullets out. The bullets are nothing but negative statements. Like an Uzi machine gun, she spews out negative and disparaging words, recklessly wounding her intended targets and any innocent bystanders that happen to be around.

Also while I was living at Love and Charity, there was another incident. There have been several people who had come in to volunteer. They had done some great work for Love and Charity, but my mother's negative face runs people away. I can recall during the day I was there and one of my mother's friends was there. She was talking about a death she had read about in the newspaper. She knew this woman who had died, and she said to my mother, "Well, that's sad to hear about that lady passing away."

My mom said to her, "You know what? When I die, people are going to be surprised."

Her friend said, "Why? About what?"

"Because I am going to be lying in the casket. Everybody is going to think that I'm dead, and you know what is going to happen? I'm going to rise up."

That woman said, "Mrs. Hunter, if you rise from that casket, everybody is going to run like hell."

I said, "I'm especially gonna run like hell if you rise from that casket." I believe in my heart that there was only one person who rose from the dead, and that was Jesus Christ. It would be comments like this that would make people who wanted to help run away from her.

Two faces of Louise Hunter. You'll never know unless you spend time with her. If you spend time with her, you'll say that this woman is insane; this woman is incompetent. This woman has mental issues. This woman needs to be delivered. This woman is not truthful. My mother has a very effective allure. She will pull you in with her superficial, loving mother façade, but what she's really doing is sizing you up. Yes, that first impression will be so great. Then after that she will start running you away. She will say to people, "Well, he or she left because they were trying to take over my mission. They want my mission." That's what she says about people. She said that about me. I don't want her mission. I never did and never will because God hasn't put it in my heart to take over Love and Charity.

If my mother would allow me to work with her, I could turn Love and Charity into a great organization because I believe I have the skills and the vision to take the mission to the next level. In May 2012, I earned my degree in business administration. I know what it takes to turn an organization around, but I would not do it for Love and Charity because to me it is a dysfunctional organization. It's a shame that I say it, but it's the truth. It is an organization that does not have leadership or a vision. In order to be a great leader, you have to first be a good follower. You have to be willing to learn and wait your turn for leadership.

What I understand from numerous individuals that tried to work with my mother, and even from other ministries and churches, is that E was not teachable. When a person tried to teach her, she would cut them off by saying, "I get it, I get it." But really, she didn't get it. That was just her way of shutting them up so she could really go on doing what she had already been doing. She always wants to go to the next step without really taking the necessary first steps.

She would always jump, and holler, and scream, and stuff. She was always shouting on the floor, always wanting attention. She wants to be the celebrity. She wants to have the spotlight. She wants everybody looking at her. My mother has a serious "I" problem. With her it's always about "I." She's never been a team player. In my opinion, she has never been about teamwork because everything she does is, "I did this. I did that." She thinks that leadership is all about lying and being manipulative. Therefore, in the long run, her organization will fail.

In the Bible, Hosea 4:6 says that people are being destroyed because of a lack of knowledge. I think that is very true. My mother has no knowledge, none whatsoever. She doesn't even read the Bible. She doesn't even pray. She doesn't get on the phone and communicate with people. She doesn't know how to talk to people. "God called me to Love and Charity. God did it. God did it." People like my mom always say that God told them to do things. That way, no one can argue with her if God said it. This is a ruse, a pretense, and falsehood. Deep down in her heart, I believe she knows that I know that God did not call her. She called herself. She is self-appointed. She is a law unto herself which is a very dangerous thing. I find that the axiom "Power corrupts, and absolute power corrupts absolutely" is very true. My mom is the perfect example of this unfortunate truth.

It frustrates her when she looks at her son who is qualified to manage Love and Charity properly. I could do this job, but she doesn't want me to do the job. What she really wants me to do is operate the way that she does. She wants me to have two faces like she does, to be corrupt, to be dishonest, to be unfaithful. She wants me to say to the world, "Yes, I love Jesus," and then backstab, belittle, and say nasty things. Then I would say, "Oh, I didn't say that. I'm a Christian. Why would I say something like that? I'm a Christian. I would never say anything like that." Okay, Christian. Some of the most corrupt, defiled, ugly-spirited, mean people that I have met in my life have claimed to be Christians.

For example, in an article published in the *Insider News* (March 1-15, 1993), a local newspaper in Racine, a story was done on Dennis Woods after he joined Love and Charity, introducing him as a new associate director. You see, that's how my mother got Dennis to leave the ministry he was already with. My mother asked him to come help her run the mission. After he came to Love and Charity, the newspaper article came out. Evidently after this article was published, my mother got jealous and jumped down his throat, telling him that he was not an associate director. He was just a plain mission-man which was a complete contradiction of her asking him to help run the mission. As a matter of fact, she told Dennis that once she trained him, she was going to leave the mission and get an apartment which she did. However, once that article came out, she dogged Dennis' steps until he left.

One of the main problems that my mother has always had is that she can never get along with authentic Christians. Whenever real Christians attempt to join up with my mother, whether they be ministers, churches, charitable organizations, etc., one by one they come, and just as surely as they come, one by one they leave, frustrated and dismayed by my mother. Like oil and water, real Christians and my mother could never mix. The only people she can associate with are corrupt and compromised people like herself.

I remember the time when an authentic Christian came through. He never knew who I was. I was just sitting in the chapel. He was praying for people, and he called me up. He said to me, "Young man, you are going to be a powerful man of God. Your mother is going to get into some serious trouble. Even though you have no relationship with your mom, she is going to get in trouble, and you are going to be the one who saves your mom. You are going to pay all her debts off because your mother is going to get into trouble, and you are going to come help her and pay her bills off." After saying this, he asked, "Is your mom here?"

I said, "Yeah, that's my mom right there."

He said to her, "God is telling me that you are going to get into trouble. And when you get into trouble, this man, your son right here—what number son is he?"

"That's my baby son," she replied.

"He's going to help you out in a financial way. You are going to do something so stupid, and you are going to go to him, and he is going to help you out."

After service was over with, I never saw that man again. My mother was going around for a couple weeks saying, "That nigger ain't gonna help me. I ain't gonna get into trouble with nothing. That nigger ain't gonna help me do anything." That's what she said. But who knows what the future holds? Who knows? That's all I have to say. Who knows what the future holds? That's why I say you never know where your help might come from. Besides, what's wrong with a son bailing out his mother anyway? What's wrong with that is that I would have to be successful in order to fulfill that prophecy, and that's where the problem is: my mother doesn't want to see me be successful.

If you come into Love and Charity, she is waiting for you. When you walk through the doors, she is going to greet you. She is going to put a smile on her face and say, "I've been a Christian for over fifty years, and I love the Lord. I love Him with all my heart. I care for Him. Come on, let me pray for you." That's what she'll say. "The Lord wants to do something in your life. The Lord loves you, and I love you." As soon as she reels you into Love and Charity, a day or two later she will come with the negative attacks. "Now I'm going to beat you up. Now I'm going to beat you down. Now I'm going to kill you. Now I'm going to destroy you. I'm going to destroy you so bad that when you leave Love and Charity, you won't be the same. I'm going to kill you spiritually, so that you can't have any connection with God at all. By the time I'm finished with you, you won't be able to function in the world." You come to Love and Charity to get some help, but when you leave here, you'll be more messed up than ever. My mother used to always say that Love and Charity is like a gas station. You're here a little while, fill up with what you need, and keep going on down the road. However, what you really get at love and Charity is a tank of bad gas that destroys the engine a mile or so down the road!

Like the Bible says, the devil comes to steal, to kill, and destroy. And that's what she came to do. She came to steal, to kill, and destroy. She doesn't want you to have anything. She doesn't want you to have anything, especially more than she has.

So, beware, enter her shelter with caution. Don't let imagery like the picture depicted in *Ebony* magazine with her standing with outstretched hands under the Love and Charity sign fool you. Though the sign might say Love and Charity, there is no love. There is no charity. There is only Louise Hunter, and the god created in her own image.

Divide and Conquer

Ever since I came into this world, I began to understand my mother's attitude, her behavior, and her actions. My mother loved having my sisters and brothers arguing with each other, having them go against each other. She would say things to one child, then go back and tell the other child what the first child had allegedly said. Some of my brothers and sisters would fight physically or verbally. As a child, I thought that was very wrong because a mother should not divide a family up to conquer. What did she want to conquer? I witnessed a lot of fights between my brothers and sisters. My mom would sit back and laugh.

My sisters and brothers shared a lot of information. My sister Bonnie would say that Dad used to say, "If anything ever happens to me, remember that brothers and sisters stick together. Do not allow your mother to divide you guys up." Bonnie always used to say that my dad would say that my mother was crazy. My brother James was always the black sheep of the family. My mom constantly got on him saying bad things to my brothers and sisters about him. My brothers and sisters used to confront him. He would say, "No, I did not say that. No, I did not do that. She's lying." My mother is very good at orchestrating a lie and standing by the lie, then watching family members—sisters and brothers, cousins, nieces and nephews, aunties and uncles—fight with each other. She's very good at that.

Whenever we used to get into an argument about the structure of Love and Charity, my mother would tell my brothers and sisters, "You know Paul always hated me. You know he never liked me. You know he wants to take over Love and Charity. And y'all know that if he takes over Love and Charity, y'all wouldn't be able to come here and get bread, cereal, milk, and all the stuff that comes in to Love and Charity." Some of my brothers and sisters believed that, and some of them didn't.

I used to argue with my brothers and sisters and tell them adamantly, "I do not want Love and Charity." I used to tell them, "My major is business administration. I want to be in business to make a profit, not run a not-for-profit corporation."

I remember the time a resident named Randy was living there, as well as Chris, Richard, and a couple other residents. She used to have Randy go to Milwaukee to pick up food. Randy would do it. Then when the food got back, she would have him unload the truck and take the food into the shelter. She would call them over one by one. She would say, "Randy, watch Chris because I think he is selling my meat. I think he is sneaking my meat out of the shelter and selling it." Five minutes later, she would call Chris over and say, "Chris, I want you to watch Randy because I believe he is stealing my meat, so I want you to watch him. Somebody called the shelter and told me that Randy was stealing my meat." She would call Richard over and say the same thing to him, and then call another resident and say the same thing to him.

This happened consistently at Love and Charity. Just imagine these men and women that she was dividing up to conquer. I don't even know why. They were looking at each other, watching each other, and she was sitting back laughing because that's what the devil's daughter does—sits back and laugh. "Ha ha ha, I got y'all. Y'all looking at each other." That's what my mom is all about, divide and conquer. It's all about her. What can you do for me? She's a woman who's on a mission to divide families, to divide friendships, to divide anybody up. She will lie about you. She will steal from you. She will take anything from you because she is a divider. She's not a unifier.

Mom, why do you want to do this? Why do you want to cause pain to your family members? Why? My mother would insist that our aunts and uncles never liked us; they always hated us. She warned, "Don't go around them. They never did like y'all." They always wanted to see us when we were children, but she had poisoned our minds. As we became adults and we began to go visit them, they showed us nothing but love. They never showed dislike or hate. She poisoned our minds when we were children, but now that we are adults and we sit back and analyze, we say, "Mom, you were wrong."

Mom gave up her first daughter, Elizabeth Strong. She was adopted by my mother's parents. She was wrong to give her up, but she has never apologized.

There is nothing wrong with coming to your son or your daughter and asking for forgiveness. It's easy to go to God and say, "God, forgive me. I'm sorry."

When Louise Hunter is deceased, she claims that her children will not be left in her will or named as beneficiaries on her insurance. The insurance policy is paid faithfully each month, but the people who are going to benefit from the policy are just three of her pick. Only one of her sixty-one grandchildren and two of her fifty-five or more great-grandchildren are beneficiaries. On several occasions E has been emphatic about not leaving "a dime" to her children, including me. This is one more action that demonstrates how she really feels about her kids, despite having dragged us through hell establishing and maintaining Love and Charity.

In my opinion, you should not leave inheritance money to anyone who is unproductive and living questionable lifestyles. Whenever drugs or alcohol are involved, receiving a sudden windfall only exacerbates the problem, and that money often does more harm than good. Evidently that does not concern her insofar as the ones she chose, but she might want to take a closer look. Such favoritism is often found in many families, but in ours, it only pits the grandchildren's and great-grandchildren's generations against mine. Once again, E orchestrates dividing and conquering.

There is a possibility that others could be added as beneficiaries on her insurance who are not living questionable lifestyles, but we will only know that for certain when that day comes.

I remember reading a book that said that the most difficult thing to overcome is spiritual abuse. Spiritual abuse strips away individuality, destroys self-esteem, and damages the very core of a person—their soul. And whenever someone abuses someone else's soul, it's downright evil. Looking back at the emotional abuse and neglect that my mother perpetrated upon her own children, it really is appropriate that she insists that we call her E. Because after years of experiencing my mother's two faces, it is undeniably clear that "E" stands for evil.

CHAPTER 7

A Hard Day's Work

One thing that I learned at an early age is that if you wanted to get ahead in life, it would take endurance and hard work. I was hired at Taco Bell at the age of sixteen. I remember that I had to get a work permit from the Urban League. I had to have my mother take me to get the work permit. She didn't want to do it. On the way to get that work permit she complained all the way there. She told me, "I do not have time for this. I have to do the Lord's will." She would say that all the time, "I have to do the Lord's will." Nevertheless, she reluctantly took me. She signed the papers, and I countersigned, and they issued the work permit.

I loved that Taco Bell job. I think anyone's first job is an unforgettable milestone in his or her life. I had a great time there, but I had to quit because my mother didn't want to be responsible for taking me to work, and often she wouldn't.

A year later, I started to work at Burger King, which was one block away from my house on Douglas Avenue. I loved that job too because I learned how to cook, making burgers and fries. I'd put the burgers through the machine and watch them come out the other end. It was a great job for me. I learned valuable interpersonal communications skills, customer service, how to get along with my co-workers, and work together as a team.

When I became eighteen years old, I ended up working for Warren Industries. That was a tough place to work for any American. It was very difficult. I stayed busy. In order to use the bathroom, I would have to raise my hand until the supervisor recognized me and came to relieve me so that I could go to the restroom. I didn't stay at that job long because it was too labor-intensive.

After Warren Industries, I ended up working for Racine Unified. I worked for Unified for a couple years. I started off as a hall monitor at McKinley Middle School. I enjoyed working with the kids, monitoring the hallways and the outside of the facility. I had to make sure the teenagers did not get into any physical altercations or any mischief like smoking on school grounds. I ended up leaving Unified due to some dramatic changes in my life.

As was my pattern, I would work a couple jobs here and there and then quit because I was receiving SSI. My next job was at the Racine Detention Center. I stayed on that job for about a year or so. That's when I discovered it wasn't for me. I wanted to do something. I decided to go back to school. I enrolled at Gateway Technical College.

Another job was at Chrysler Engine Plant starting in 2008 and ending in January 2010. I liked the job. It was first shift. I enjoyed working with the people, but I just didn't like the union at all. The union is not what it used to be. I was an assembly worker. They discharged me for attendance because I had to make an appearance in court. I had to appear in court, so I also had to accept the consequences. However, in the meantime I discovered that I qualified for the T.R.A. program because Chrysler had shut down. That's where the company pays for you to go back to school to be retrained. I already had my associate's degree, so I decided to go back and get my bachelor's degree. I enrolled at Upper Iowa University. I used the T.R.A. program to get my bachelor's degree in business administration, so being employed at Chrysler helped provide a way for me to continue my education.

Of all the jobs that I have had, I know in my heart that all my previous jobs were just transition positions because I have a deep yearning to own my own business. I believe that all of the experiences that I have encountered up to now are preparing me for the eventuality that I will, one day, be the president and CEO of a business that I start. One of the things that I have a knack for is public relations. Therefore, I would like to own my own P.R. firm. This is something that I enjoy and which I am good at.

For years, I helped my mother around the mission by setting up speaking engagements and helping her coordinate fundraiser events with various business entities and even celebrities. I worked closely with several Racine corporations, such as Johnson Products, the Racine Police Department, the Mayor's office, and the *Racine Journal Times* newspaper. However, once my mother's book, *Love and Charity*, came out, I was the sole source for arranging all of the media coverage. Beside getting my mother and the author, Dennis Woods, booked on local news shows in Milwaukee, I also had them booked on national television programs, magazines, and radio broadcasts. It was simply unbelievable that with my determination and persistence, my mother's face was seen all over the country and her amazing story talked about all over the world. That's right, around the world! One of our Associated Press new releases was picked up by a newspaper in Japan! I know that I can be an effective leader. I just need the chance.

Halo, the New Shelter in Town

A few years ago, an organization named Halo opened up a homeless shelter here in Racine. Halo was a multi-million-dollar, state-of-the-art homeless shelter that had several programs to assist those in need. They had plenty of resources and funding from multiple sources, including state and federal government entities. Once Halo opened up, they were hiring for several positions. At the time, I had an apartment, and I applied and got hired. That was right around the same time that a former Love and Charity resident named Chris was also hired. I could only work at Halo for a short time, two or so weeks. The first week was the most difficult week that I have ever experienced at a job.

One day, a young, pregnant caucasian lady who was dating an African-American man came to Halo looking for a place to stay. Before Halo, she had lived at Love and Charity for a week during the same time that Chris was still there. While there, my mother had gotten on this young lady about her association and relationship with a black man, saying, "You pregnant by that black man? Shouldn't no white woman be pregnant by a black man." That racist statement that she made was totally disrespectful and inappropriate. The young lady was completely undone, so she decided to leave Love and Charity and come over to Halo.

After getting registered, the young lady saw Chris and me working in the office. She started crying. She went to talk to her counselor. Her counselor came in and talked to us. Then she came in and said, "You know how Mrs. Hunter treated me, Chris. She's a racist. She asked me, 'Why are you pregnant by that black man? Shouldn't no white woman be pregnant by a black man.'

You know she said that, Chris. You were standing right there."

Chris couldn't do anything but tell the truth. After Chris and I got off from work around eleven-thirty, we were walking home. I asked Chris, "Did that really happen at Love and Charity?"

Chris said, "Yes, it did."

I said, "You were there when my mom said that to that girl?"

He said, "Yeah, but there's nothing I can do, Paul, because if I would have said something, she would have put me out."

I said, "Wow."

Hearing that incident blew me away. I worked at Halo for two weeks before I quit because the people who used to live at Love and Charity were now living at Halo, and I got tired of them saying, "Your mama is Satan's daughter." They would ask, "Why are you working here when your mom has that homeless shelter? You should be over there working with her." Female residents at Halo were saying this. They were telling me how they disliked my mother and informing me that she is going to hell for some of the things that she has done. I could not disagree with them. I believe in my heart that if my mother does not ask the Lord for forgiveness for the things that she has said and done to people, she faces God's judgment. The Bible does say in Matthew 25:40-41, "Truly, I say to you, as you did it to one of the least of these my brothers, you did it to me. Then shall he say also unto them on the left hand, Depart from me, ye cursed, into everlasting fire, prepared for the devil and his angels."

During my short time at Halo, there were consistent derogatory statements regarding my mother. They would say something every day throughout the eight-hour shift, and it was always negative. Sometimes I used to just smile, but I felt very uncomfortable. When I analyzed the situation, I would say, "My mother has done more harm than good to the residents of Love and Charity." I decided to resign from Halo because it was very uncomfortable working there. I just couldn't take it anymore.

Many people—not knowing that I was Louise Hunter's son—would make negative statements to me about Love and Charity and my mother. People were saying that they hoped Love and Charity would close down. They even made statements like they wished my mom would die. That was very upsetting and scary to hear people say things like that. Halo taught me that you need to treat people the way you want to be treated.

The word had gotten out about my mother and Love and Charity. Not too long ago, an article came out in the *Racine Journal Times* that my mother needed money to keep the gas service on. At the end of the online version of the article, there was a link where you could see all the comments people were making about the story about Love and Charity's gas bill. There were pages of very nasty and negative comments about my mom, Love and Charity, and even about some of my relatives. It was shocking and embarrassing to see what many of Racine's residents were saying about Love and Charity.

But, you know what? Looking back on it, they were absolutely right. She comes off as a nice person, but once you walk into the doors of Love and Charity, she's a divider, not a unifier. Yes, we all have issues. We all have problems, but the God that I serve does not divide people up. The God that I serve is a unifier. The God that I serve is love. The God that I serve shows compassion. The God that I serve is a great God. He's a caring God, a loving God, a patient God. He shows kindness. He gives me happiness. He looks after me. He protects me. The God that I serve is an almighty God. The God that I serve does not put me down. The God that I serve is sweet. The God that I serve has my back and will always be there for me.

So, Louise Hunter, I pray that God will really touch your heart, mind, and spirit, and bring you back to the Body of Christ where you belong because what you are doing is totally wrong. You cannot serve two masters. Remember those words. You either hate one and love the other, or despise one and cling to the other, but you cannot serve two. My question to you, Louise Hunter, is, "Who do you serve?"

CHAPTER 8

A Mission in Decline

I remember when I was a child, Love and Charity Homeless Shelter had some great ideas for homeless people in the City of Racine. Love and Charity started off as a nonprofit organization. It was one of the first homeless shelters established in Racine. My mother had told people that God gave her a vision to open up a homeless shelter for residents in Racine which was a good thing because at the time Love and Charity was organized, there were people on the board who were very informed. I remember former Mayor Jim Smith, a prominent clergyman, a lady who worked at Parkside University, and others all served on Love and Charity's Board of Directors.

One aspect of the structure that the mission had was the rules and the routine that my mom had developed. A few of these rules were that residents had to get up at seven a.m. They had to do their chores. After their chores, they had breakfast and then they had to leave and could not return until five-thirty p.m. I thought it was great because it encouraged them to be productive, finding employment and not sitting around and free-loading all day. The residents at that time loved it. They would get up in the morning and complete their as-signed chores and go out to find a job; some of them did get hired by local businesses. Once they saved up some money for three to six months, they would move out im-mediately.

However, as time passed, I began to see a change in how my mother was handling things. All of a sudden she did not like her board members. What it really was, she did not want educated people on her board, and soon they started to disappear. The reason was because my mother had this attitude that it was her way or no way at all.

My mother wanted to have the right to shove church down people's throats whether they wanted it or not. I watched countless services where residents were in attendance. When my mother wanted them to pray, they had to pray. When she wanted them to sing and clap, she made them sing and clap. The poor residents felt that they had no choice, so they did it to get it over with, but this method rarely netted an authentic reli-gious experience. Usually the only one that received any gratification from her services was her because she was bolstering her own ego and building an empire on the backs of emotionally fragile residents who came to Love and Charity seeking help.

Then, you also had the issue that some of the peo-ple that came to the mission were of different religious backgrounds and faiths. Some were Catholic, Lutheran, Presbyterian, Methodist, Baptist, and Pentecostal. Of course, some were even atheists and agnostics. How-ever, since my mother describes herself as a Pentecostal, to her that was the only denomination that existed. She wanted everybody to do things the way Pentecostals do things. That would mean all these non-Pentecostals were very uncomfortable during her worship services.

Imagine someone trying to force you to worship God outside of your own worship experience. Imagine someone attempting to make you speak in tongues and forcing you to scream and shout when you were used to quiet, reverent praise and worship. None of that made a difference to my mother. She really didn't care what you thought or how you had done it in the past; it was either her way or the highway.

This whole idea of a forced Pentecostal experience is practically a contradiction in terms. According to the Bible, you *receive* the Holy Ghost. You do not have him forced on you. I bring this up because there were many times that I witnessed my mother trying to make someone get the Holy Ghost. And, the way she did it was, she made them say thank you Jesus, thank you Jesus, thank you Jesus, repeatedly until they worked themselves into an ecstatic state. People would end up speaking gibberish which was often interpreted as speaking in tongues. If they didn't do it the way she said, they would be threatened with being put out of the mission.

Another thing E would impose on mission residents is she would tell them, "I need you to go down in the office and type a letter. I need you to get on the phone and get donations." With current residents, she would threaten, "I'll put you out if you don't do what I want you to do." So, they had to go along with her or get put out. Imagine that. Here you are homeless with nowhere to go, and you're forced to do what she says under the threat of being told to leave.

As E continued getting full of herself, she came up with all kinds of bizarre rules. You could not have a cell phone, and once you got into Love and Charity, you would have ten days inside before you could leave to go look for a job. It's what she called probation. You could go look for a job after ten days, but not before. If you complete your ten-day "probation," she would say, "You stayin' right here. I don't care what the rules say. You stayin' right here or you can leave if you don't like it. You don't need no job. What you need is Jesus. You need to stay busy around here working."

My mother works these residents like slaves. She gets them up at five-thirty a.m. They can't have breakfast until she says, "Okay, it's time for you to have breakfast. You can go cook you something to eat. Okay, you can have some lunch. Okay, you can have dinner now." She's a dictator. If it's time for them to go upstairs and go to bed, she says, "Nope, you wait on me. I tell you when to go." She will just sit in the kitchen until around nine-thirty, ten o'clock, sometimes eleven o'clock, then say, "Okay, let's go on upstairs."

I'm going to share some of these rules with you.

Rule one: Ten days is normal probation. During this time there is no leaving the building. Probation is thirty days for people with suspected drug and alcohol problems, but they go against this rule also.

Rule two: Residents must be dressed and downstairs by five-thirty a.m. during the weekdays and seven a.m. on the weekends. Residents comply with this rule.

Rule three: No one goes to his or her room without Mother Hunter's permission. People get up at five-thirty a.m. and work sixteen to seventeen hours a day. She tries to keep the residents busy because she believes that if they stay busy, their minds are not going to wander off thinking about drugs and alcohol or doing something stupid.

There have been times when residents were extremely physically, mentally, and spiritually tired. This woman would not allow them to go back to their rooms. This process eventually would wear down anyone's resistance. Just imagine getting up at five-thirty. You could be sick, but you were still coming down those steps, and she was still going to work you. You're working like a slave, and worst of all, you're not going to be compensated one red cent. The way she sees it, "I'm giving you room and board and food, so we're going to work you." Some of these women and guys did it for a period of time. Then, they had to go, "I can't take this anymore."

Rule four: No phone or internet. That means that they can't have a cell phone and they cannot use the internet at Love and Charity. Hold up! She is here to help people, not immobilize them. This rule is upsetting. What if family calls? What if the residents want to call mom or dad for the holidays? What if they want to get on the internet and look for a job?

Rule five: No drugs or alcohol.

Rule six: No food in the room.

Rule seven: Residents must cancel all AODA appointments. I don't think that rule should be in there. If people want to go to AODA meetings to maintain their sobriety, they should be allowed to go. However, E wasn't having it. She would say, "You are going to stay here. God is going to deliver you. You don't need those meetings. You don't need those appointments. My God is going to heal you. All you need to do is listen to me, watch me, learn from me."

Rule eight: No stealing or cursing.

Rule nine: No going downstairs after bed, or the alarm will go off.

Love and Charity Homeless Shelter in Racine, Wisconsin, has had many people walk through its doors. Whites, Blacks, Hispanics, Chinese, all different kinds of people. It has been very diverse. Some of the people were very highly educated. These people taught me how to use proper English. They taught me how to be articulate. The relationship that I had with them was great because I learned never to do drugs and alcohol because you can become addicted to them. They used to tell me all the time that it might start off fun, but as you continue to do it, it becomes an addiction where you need it every day. I have seen school teachers, lawyers, school principals, assembly line workers, people in the medical field, professional and non-professional people walk through the doors of Love and Charity. I developed relationships with them, and it was great because I was able to analyze their lives and say to myself, I do not want to live this type of life. I do not want to become addicted to drugs and alcohol.

Some of our residents that had fallen on hard times actually came from rich families and middle-class families. In retrospect, what I learned from these people is to be the best that you can be and associate with winners, not losers. If you hang around losers, that is where you are going to end up. I learned to always surround myself with positive people who are going places.

To this day, I stay in touch with people who lived at Love and Charity. They have moved on in their lives, even though E mistreated most of them; they never held it against me. They just kept on moving and did not look back.

CHAPTER 9

My *Unplanned* Parenthood

When I was twenty-two or twenty-three, I had my own apartment. I was young and full of energy. My friends and nephews used to come over and bring girls. I remember the time when I met the mother of my children at my house. Keep in mind that a lot of other women were in and out of my house because back then I still had that player mentality and just wanted to have fun. She came to my house with her friends. While she was at the house, I began to have a conversation with her. At first, I didn't really like her, but we conversed. At that time, I wanted to set her up with my nephew, but I didn't. As we began to talk, I had a great conversation with her. I remember saying to her, "You should go to the store with me."

She said, "Okay, I'll walk to the store with you."

I remember that as we were going out the door, I asked her to go down into the basement with me. We went to the basement and had sex there. The first time that I had sex with her, she got pregnant. She conceived my child. Once I found out that she was pregnant, I was afraid, and bewildered. I didn't know what I was going to do. She was scared too. I remember that when she told me that she was pregnant, my head dropped. I remember crying, "What am I going to do? A child that I fathered is coming into this world in the next nine months." I was frightened.

Her reaction to me was awesome. At first, it was just a great time that we had together, communicating and interacting with each other, doing little stuff. We had a great time with that. Her reaction to me was, "Let's have a relationship. I'm pregnant. You are the father of this child. Let's have this family together." Her reaction was great. I loved her.

I think the magic really happened when I knew that she was pregnant, and I wanted to be there with my child. I wanted to be a part of my child's life in any capacity because my father died in a car crash when I was eight years old. I wanted to be a father to my child. My first child—I was so excited. In the past when I had engaged in sexual activity, I always believed that I couldn't have children, but it was a magical moment when I looked into my daughter's eyes for the first time.

Once that woman had the baby, I tried to have a monogamous relationship. I tried to win her over by trying to be faithful and honest with her, but I just couldn't. I tried to be a man who was going to be there with her and support her in any way (emotionally, physically, and spiritually). I think that I won her over because I was a person who didn't drink, didn't do drugs, wasn't into the bar scene or hanging out. I think that was an acceptable compromise on her part because I didn't have all the other baggage.

The first child I had was Jenna. The second one was Victoria. The third one was Isaiah. The fourth one was by another woman. I do not know his name because the mother would not share it with me. I am the father of four children. I love all my children from the bottom of my heart and would do anything for them.

Margarita, the mother of my first three children, is a good woman, but she had a problem with letting me be the man of the house. At times she could be mean, hateful, conniving, and deceiving. One of the big problems I had with her was that she refused to tell the truth and was manipulative. But that was her. She had her shortcomings, and I'm sure if you asked her, she could give a list of my dirty laundry too.

My first child is Jenna Lynn Hunter. She was born on January 28, 1994. The first child is very unique. On the day she was born, I was excited and overwhelmed. I went to the hospital. I held her in my arms. I remember that day clearly. The day she was born, the San Francisco 49ers were in the Super Bowl. I was ecstatic about having my daughter being born the day the 49ers were in the Super Bowl. I took a picture with her. I remember crying. She's my daughter, and I love her. I remember being with her from when she was small all the way until now.

My daughter Jenna is a talented and gifted person. When she really works hard and decides to apply herself (giving one hundred percent instead of giving fifty percent), she is awesome. She's wonderful. She's beautiful. She has a great demeanor about herself. She's always calm and collected. She's a great speaker and is very articulate. I envy that sometimes because I say to myself, "She does not get that from me. She must have gotten it from her mother's side of the family." I think she will go far in life because she is such a great communicator.

My second child is Victoria Marie Hunter. She was born on February 17, 1997. She's very athletic. She's very good when it comes to sports, particularly basketball. I remember when she was born, she was a real crybaby. I remember being at the hospital when she was born. Then I had to go to work at Racine Unified afterward. The day she was born, I cried. I was happy. I said, "Another daughter. Lord, why are you giving me these daughters? I want a son." But whatever He gave me, I was happy and said thank you for these precious gifts from God. I'm thankful because they came out good, healthy, and strong.

Victoria struggles when it comes to academics, but I would constantly tell her all the time that without struggle, there is no progress—no pain, no progress. I tell her all the time that she needs to raise her hand in class and never be afraid to ask the teacher a question. I always say to her, "You need to sit in the front row. Most students who sit in the front row are very effective. They stay alert, and they pass with As or Bs. Always sit in the front row and never be afraid to ask for help. That's how you improve, and, besides, there are no dumb questions because you are there to learn."

Victoria is a very good basketball player. She comes across as a person who is disarming, and she will befriend you. However, when she steps onto the basketball court, you are no longer her friend. It's strictly competitor against competitor. As Victoria begins to improve academically and athletically, she is going to be a formidable opponent and a winner. Like Jenna, she is a very good speaker. My girls like to joke, just like their father. I remember a time when I used to hide and they would walk past me. Then I would jump out and say boo. They would jump. They do that to me now, all three of them. It's just fun.

My third child is my first son, Isaiah Joseph Muñoz Hunter. He was born on October 29, 1998. I was excited about him just like I was with the rest of them. I said, "Wow, I can't believe that I finally have a son. Now I can do some guy things with him. I can teach him some things about life that I never had the opportunity to learn from my father. As he becomes older, I can teach him how to play football, how to read, how to write, how to play sports. As they get bigger, I am going to coach them for any sport. My son Isaiah and I have a lot in common. He's a calm, collected guy. He's tough mentally, and he doesn't let people get to him easily. He is studious, a quick learner, and great academically. I don't know where he gets his smarts from because he certainly doesn't get them from me.

I do not know anything about my fourth child. He took his mother's last name. I was in a relationship with his mom. What happened was I met his mom at the YMCA. We first became friends and then it led to sex. I had sex with her about seven times. She ended up having a son by me. I had this relationship with Melanie because I was in an abusive relationship with Margarita. She didn't want me to interact with my child, but as a father, I feel that I should have the ability to interact with my son. He was born on March 17, 2003, on St. Patrick's Day. I never met him because his mother doesn't want him to know me. I would like to know if he is my son or not. I will find out by requesting a paternity test. I don't have a great relationship with the mom, but I would love to have a relationship with the child, so I want to know if he is mine. I am going to find out where she lives, and I am going to take her to court to see if he is mine. If he is mine, I am going to take care of my child, just like I do the rest of my children. I want to have a relationship with all of my children. Besides, there will come a time in my child's life when he will want to know who his father is, and I want to be there for him when that time comes.

I think the milestones were when my kids came into this world. I was happy. It was just like winning the lottery. It was like being on top of the Empire State Building. It was like winning a heavyweight championship in boxing. It was like beating up Mike Tyson. Their births were milestones. I told my children I would train them to win championships in the classroom and on the basketball court. I had learned that you have to see it, believe it, and go out and achieve it. I planted positive seeds into my children. I wanted to do that so they could be winners and achieve success in their lives.

The Greatest Kids in the World!
Jenna, Paul, Victoria and Isaiah
Photo provided by Paul Hunter

CHAPTER 10

The Joys of Parenthood

I recall when each one of my children was born. I remember each milestone like it was yesterday. It was so fulfilling to see when my kids first began to explore the world around them. I remember when Jenna started crawling. I was so happy to see this. With each new thing that a newborn does, it's like a celebration. "Yes, she's crawling the first time." She was a fast crawler. I mean she'd get away from you if you didn't watch her. Jenna's quickness coincides with her personality, a quick-witted person, constantly moving. On the other hand, my daughter Victoria was a little bit slower. Victoria has a lower-key personality. When it comes to Isaiah, he too, was lower-key, but developmentally they both did just fine.

The interaction that I have had with my children was always physical, verbal, and affectionate. Unlike my mother, who never hugged us or told us how much she loved us, I was openly verbal and affectionate with them by hugging them, wrestling on the floor with them, tickling them, doing daddy's little things with them. I loved it, and so did they. I miss that interaction with them today. Every father and mother always reminisces about those precious times when children are growing, the fun play things that you did together. The simplicity and dynamics of parent-child interactions and bonding are so precious. The innocence of early childhood brings a joy that never gets old.

I often smile when I reminisce about being in the grocery store with my kids and having them ask me, "Dad, can I have this? Can I have that?" I also loved it when we went on outings like the zoo together. I loved to see their little eyes light up when they saw the monkeys swinging in their cages or making funny noises as they played with one another. Then, of course, there were the times I would take my kids to the beach and play in the water and build castles in the sand. All these were the precious memories and joys of parenthood.

I remember when my Jenna was in the first grade, assisting her with learning her ABCs and her arithmetic. I really enjoyed helping my children complete their homework. This was important to me because I wanted them to learn how to solve problems. I constantly remind them, "Think it out. I'm not going to sit here and do your homework for you. You are going to have to do it yourself."

It's interesting to note in watching kids grow up that they each have their own strengths and weaknesses. For example, when it came to math, Victoria seemed to struggle the most. After her teacher wrote us a letter stating that Victoria was struggling with math, I remember going to Walgreens to get her some flashcards that could help her memorize things like her multiplication tables. I gladly took the initiative as a father to assist her because I wanted to see my baby succeed. I knew she could do it, so every evening after dinner we used to sit at the table and study together. It was all repetition, over and over again. I used to tell Victoria, "Don't be afraid to ask questions. Ask your teacher if she can assist you with your academics during lunch time."

It was great being involved with my kids' education. When I was in school my mother didn't help me with my homework because she was always too busy caring for strangers at the mission. Besides, even if she wasn't doing that, she is functionally illiterate and could not have helped anyway. Therefore, having had those kinds of experiences, I certainly didn't want that for my children, so I invested the time to make sure they could reach their full potential. That's why the teacher sent that note home because Victoria wasn't functioning academically at the level she could be. Whatever it took, I wanted them to succeed academically.

Looking back on it, I realize that it's the small things in life that are so important. Things like sitting down and eating a meal together with your family is very important. I remember cooking for my kids when they were small. All three of my kids loved breakfast, and they loved eggs. They could eat eggs twenty-four hours a day if I allowed them to do it. In the morning right before they went to school, they would say, "Dad, could you cook us some eggs?" I would scramble their eggs with lots of cheese and put them on wheat toast. Boy, they'd eat those egg sandwiches up so quickly and would want more. How I wish those days would come back. My children never forgot those precious times either. Years later, after my children moved to San Antonio, I went to visit them. I got up early in the mornings to fix them their scrambled eggs with cheese and wheat toast. They loved it so much. I remember Isaiah said, "Dad, I miss your eggs." That really warmed my heart.

Approximately one month after Jenna was born, I was coaching a basketball team called the Nets. Sharif Chambers, Jeremie Lackey, and Bryan Bedford were the superstars on that team, and the other players were key factors in the overall success of the team. However, 1994 was the year that our team won the championship game. This was a stunning victory and a thrilling moment for us all because we started off the season being the underdogs. While we basked in the glow of victory, Jenna was right there up in the stands. After the game, I went to the mother of my children. I gave her a kiss and kissed my daughter on the cheek. I said to my daughter, "I can't wait until you get big because I'm going to coach you in basketball."

With all of my kids, I had the opportunity to coach them in basketball. I remember when Jenna, Victoria, and Isaiah were all small. We used to walk up to Chavez Community Center during the summertime, and I would teach them some of the fundamentals of basketball. I would have a basketball in their hands. I would say, "Dribble with your right hand for this block. Next block, dribble with your left hand." They hated dribbling with their left hand. I used to tell them, "I'm a basketball coach. I'm not going to work on your strengths. I'm going to work on your weaknesses. That's been my philosophy, strengthening your weaknesses." I used to set up cones at Chavez Community Center and have them dribble in and out of cones. Some of the staff used to say, "You are expecting too much from your kids. The ability to play basketball will come later on in life."

I said, "No, I want them to learn it now. That way, they can be different from anybody else, and no one will be able to take the ball from them." This is an important lesson in life on or off the court. Control the ball, and don't let anyone take it from you.

I remember when we would get to Chavez Community Center, I wouldn't let Isaiah dribble. I would tell him, "Sit down and have a seat because you can't do this drill." I would have Jenna and Victoria do it. He would be crying, "I want to do it. I know I can do it."

I said, "Okay, I'm going to let you do it." I would look at this little four-year-old dribbling the basketball, and I was amazed how he dribbled the ball in and out of the cones. He was doing better than the girls, and they were older than he was. I began to think, "I can't wait until you get in first grade. Then I'm going to coach you in basketball."

I love teaching my kids to play basketball as a way to teach them about life. I started to plant seeds in them. I told them that when they played Optimist basketball, they were going to win championships. I remember that they developed their skills extremely well. Jenna was in the eighth grade. Victoria was in the fourth grade, but she was on the fifth-grade basketball team. Both of them were in the championship that year. I was just amazed. I remember taking them to the YMCA. I said, "Jenna, I've been coaching basketball for years. If you would just listen to me, you can help your team win the championship." I wasn't coaching her then. She had another coach. I said, "Jenna, this is what I think is going to play out. Your team is undefeated. I think this is what's going to happen. It's going to be a close game. I believe that you are going to get the ball. This is what you need to work on. When you get the ball and you dribble, put the ball in your left hand and dribble, then cross it over to your right hand if someone steps in front of you. Then drive all the way to the basket, looking to pass. If you can't pass, shoot it."

Jenna gave me a hard time that day because she didn't want to do the drills at the YMCA. However, I wanted her to practice that scenario so she would know what to do when it was game time. Before playing any game, it is important that the team does its warm-up drills. The drill consisted of ten free throws, twenty layups with the right hand, twenty with the left hand, and then some dribbling. After I was finished drilling them, I took them over to Chavez Community Center to get a feel for the atmosphere and get ready for the game.

The first game was Victoria's. She was a fourth-grader. The game went all the way down to the wire. Victoria's team ended up going into overtime. It came down to free throws. I remember that the game was tied, and Victoria ended up taking the ball from a girl. She was fouled. She made both her free throws. Then it was the other team's turn. They got the ball with about twenty to thirty seconds left. They attempted to score and turned the ball over. Victoria grabbed the ball and ran the clock out. They won the championship. I was happy for her because I always told her that they were going to win the championship. I was the third assistant coach for that team. I remember telling the coach, "I've been coaching for years. If you want to go to the championship, this is what you want to do. When you get in the playoff, you double-team them. When that player comes in with the ball, double-team her. When their players pass half court, double-team them. Wait until the playoff to do it." He did it, and we went to the championship and won by two points. It was great because that strategy worked.

The last game was at five-thirty p.m. It was Jenna's team. They were trying to make history. They were undefeated. It was a good game, a close game. They lost by five points. They could have won the game. Jenna got a rebound and dribbled it up the court. A girl stepped in front of her, Jenna ran her over, and they called an offensive foul. The other team got the ball and scored. Then they ran out the clock and won by five points.

After the game, I told Jenna, "It was a good game. Keep your head up. Remember what I told you at the YMCA? If somebody comes at you while you're dribbling, cross over."

She said, "Yes, Dad, and I forgot."

I said, "That's all right. You're still a winner to me."

Years have passed. My son was in first grade. I signed him up for the Optimist league and put him on the second-grade team. I had the opportunity to coach him. We were a young team. That first year, we won only three games. But before I started coaching the Magic, the team that the Racine Optimists gave me, I told the parents from day one, "Listen here. We are not going to be a good team at all this year if we don't improve in a few areas. The only thing that I can guarantee your sons is an opportunity to go to the championship game and win by the time they reach the fifth grade."

Some of the parents thought I was crazy for making a prophecy that their kids were going to the championship when they got in fifth grade, but I said that to them. At the end of the season, we had won about three games, and we finished in last place. We weren't a good team. We had one superstar on the team. That was Lamontae Lewis. The kid was unbelievable. He was a talented basketball player and had the potential to become a great athlete. However, at the end of the season, some parents took their kids off my team. I discovered the reason why they took them off the team was because of what I had said about us not being a good team, but we would be a team that would make progress every year.

One of the difficult jobs a coach has is being able to accurately assess his team and the players' abilities. It's important to be realistic and not grandiose. If your team lacks ability and talent, you have to focus on their development and bring them up to where they can become a winning team. But I guess those parents who withdrew their sons from my team didn't understand this. However, there are no shortcuts you can take to become a champion. For example, Lamontae Lewis was a level ten player. However, my son Isaiah was at a level one. He was the only first-grader on the team. The rest of them were all second-graders. As a team, they all needed to be at level ten in order to compete for the championship. Each year that I coached the Magic team, we made progress. We ended up picking up Samad Qawi, Ari Antreassian, Daveon Clark, Shane Olsen, Keymone Harris, and Trevor George. His dad was

Dave George, the assistant coach of the Magic team. I could learn a thing or two from him because he had the knowledge and experience.

Once we started coaching our team, each year we started making noticeable progress. When the kids got in fifth grade, I told them, "Remember what I said. We are going to win the fifth-grade championship. In order for us to win the championship, we have to watch, listen, learn, and apply." I kept emphasizing that when they were in second, third, and fourth grades.

Once they got in the fifth grade, they started believing that they were going to win the championship. Coaches know the talent of their teams. They know that by making minor adjustments, working the system until it becomes second nature and getting players to play good defense, they can win the championship.

In 2009 we entered the playoffs. The way they do the playoffs is that they have a first-seed, a second-seed, all the way up to the eighth-seed. The Magic basketball team was the fourth-seed. We ended up winning our first game of the playoffs. After we won our first game, my kids were very excited and hyped. The following week, we had practice on a Friday, and our game was on a Saturday. They were so excited about winning their first playoff game that they didn't want to listen to me at practice. What I had to do was pull out a maneuver that Chuck Daley used to do when he was the coach of the Detroit Pistons in the '90s. I kicked everybody out of practice. I said, "You guys are out of focus. You don't want to listen to me. Go home and get prepared to lose against the Bucks tomorrow because that's what we're going to do. We're going to lose tomorrow because you guys are not taking this seriously. Go home and get prepared to lose. We have an opportunity to go to the championship game if we beat the Bucks tomorrow, but you guys are too out of focus, so go home and prepare to lose."

I was upset with everybody. I kicked everybody

out. My son was there. I jumped in the car, and did not say a word to him. I remember my assistant coach said to me, "Paul, what are you doing?"

I said, "Everybody's got to go."

"Well, I want to shoot with my son."

"Shoot with your son if you want." When I got ready to leave, I let my assistant coach know, "Don't say anything to your son when you get in your vehicle. Pretend that you're mad at him. Dave, we are getting ready to go to the championship game and win it. Watch."

I turned around and there came Lamontae Lewis' grandpa. Lamontae ended up calling him and telling him to come and get him because I put the team out of practice. I said to Lamontae's grandpa, "Listen here. We are getting ready to go to the championship game and win it. I had to do what I had to do. Don't say anything to him about me telling you that we're getting ready to win the championship game."

He said, "Okay."

I jumped in my car and went home. While in the process of going home, I never said a word to my son at all. He was trying to talk to me, but I never said a word to him. We got in the house, and he ran and told his mother what had happened. Later on that night she asked me, "Why did you kick them out?"

I said, "Listen here, woman, I'm not in the mood for anything. This team is getting ready to go to the championship and win it Sunday. All we have to do is beat the Bucks on Saturday. Then we'll be in the championship game on Sunday, and we're getting ready to win."

The next day, we got up and went over to Chavez Community Center for the basketball game. If we won that game Saturday, we would be in the championship game Sunday. As fate would have it, one of the Bucks' key players, Kai Days, did not participate in the game. We ended up beating the Bucks to go to the championship game. We beat the Bucks by seven to ten points.

My team was happy about being in the championship game. I told all the parents, "Have your child at the YMCA on Sunday early. We're going to have a light practice." The parents had them at the YMCA on Sunday at eleven-thirty.

We practiced for about half an hour. What I wanted to focus on was layups, shooting our free throws, and making sure everybody was on the same page. I told my guys, "We're going to win the championship game against the Celtics. We played them in the regular season, and we beat them by eighteen points. We're not going to beat them by eighteen points today. We're either going to win by one or two or three points, but we're not going to beat them by eighteen points."

We did our little light workout and we left. I remember that I had to give some kids a ride. I gave Lamontae, Austin, Maurice, and Daveon a ride in the van. My son was there also. On the way, I told them I was going to drop them off at Chavez Community Center. Then I was going home to get dressed, and I would meet them. Before I dropped them off at Douglas Park, I stopped at the store. Lamontae, who was experiencing some anxiety, asked me, "Coach, what if we lose?"

I said to him, "Listen, young man, when we step on that court, we're there to win. When we walk off the court, we will be winners."

My son said, "Dad, are you sure?"

I said, "Yes, I'm sure. We are going to win this game. I guarantee you."

I took them on to Chavez Community Center and dropped them off. I went to the house, changed clothes, and prayed. I told Margarita, "I'll meet you there. I'm not driving the van. I'm going to walk, to clear my head and to meditate." I had on my nice suit and I walked. I didn't live too far from Chavez Community Center, about six or seven blocks.

We got to the championship game. At about two-thirty, we took the floor. But before I got there, I was watching another team play. I noticed that about six or seven teams in the championship had on red jerseys. The majority of the championship teams had red jerseys. We wore red that year. Before we took the floor, we watched a girls' team that had on red win the championship. They were in fifth grade. They represented red, so we had to go out and represent, and that's exactly what we did.

We went up against the Celtics, who were coached by a great coach named Ricky Person. The first quarter was a struggle for us because the Celtics were beating us by nine points. The second quarter, they were beating us by seven points. At the start of the third quarter, they were beating us by seven points. The start of the fourth quarter, they were beating us by seven points. When there were about three minutes remaining in the game, they were winning by seven points. I decided to call a time out. When I called that time out, I told my guys, "This is our opportunity. This is our moment to come back and shock the world. This is our time. This is our championship. Let's go out and do it." That little talk seemed to ignite the passion to be winners in their young hearts. Now they were ready to step up to the plate and be winners.

After the refs blew the whistle and the game started, I'm telling you, we went out and tied that game up. Next minute I know, it was going back and forth. They would take the lead; we would take the lead. There was one minute left, and we were up by one. Thirty seconds left, and they were up by one. We were in the midst of an intense battle for the championship.

In the process of us exchanging baskets back and forth, I was in a spiritual realm, and God showed me, "I can give it to them. This is how they are going to react. They are going to be joyful." I saw them celebrating, happy that they had beat us. But then He said, "I can show you how you are going to react if y'all win it." I saw how God gave it to us. We ended up winning the championship twenty-nine to twenty-eight. The crowd was absolutely ecstatic. People were jumping up and down. Nikki Minaj has a song out that says, "If I can have this moment for life." It's exciting moments like these that you want to relive over and over again—the thrill of victory.

The crowd went nuts. My kids were ecstatic and some even cried. My assistant coach was jumping up and down all over the place. I was right there with him, jumping up and down too. We all joyfully experienced the thrill of victory along with our friends and relatives.

I remember looking up at the stands, looking at the Bucks' coach Shawn Stulo. He had a poker face. He and his son Chase walked out of the facility mad and upset that the Magic had won the championship. I was happy we had won because I planted a seed in my kids: if you can see it and believe it, go out and achieve it. That's what they did. We won that championship.

I remember Ray Hammermann, the director of the Chavez Community Center, and Jason Mars, the director of Humble Park Community Center, said that was one of the best games that they had ever seen. All I got was compliments from people saying, "You did an excellent job coaching that team. I thought your team were going to lose, but you came back. You stayed in there and maintained your composure, and kept fighting back until you came back and won the championship."

My son was excited about it. Everybody on the team was excited about it. That's why I tell people today, it's not how you start, it's how you finish. In life, that's the way it is.

People can call me a loser. They can call me lazy and whatever they want. One thing I can say is that we finished on top that year. My kids won that fifth-grade championship.

The Magic: 2009 Champions

Left: Head Coach, Paul Hunter (Back) Shane Olson, Austin Johnson
Maurice Hoard, Isaiah Hunter Munoz, Lamontae Lewis, Trevor
George (Bottom) Samad Qawi, Keymone Harris, Ari Antreassian,
Daveon Clark. Right: Assistant Coach Dave George
Photo by Ken Lumpkin, The Insider News

Now I'm coaching other teams. I have a fourth-grade team right now because my kids can no longer participate in Optimist since they are living in San Antonio, Texas. Another team I have now is a second-grade team. I'm the GM of the second-grade team, and the coach is Derrick Glass. The assistant coach is Terry Barnes. They're called the Celtics, and they went 7-1. The fourth-grade team is called the Raptors, and they went 7-1. Both teams are great. I also have my Magic team. They are eighth-graders, and they went 5-5. I believe that these teams can win championships if they will just listen, follow directions, and watch. They have to see it, believe it, and go out and achieve it. If they do that, we can win some games. We can be in the championship.

The Celtics

Left: Head Coach, Derrick Glass (Back) Amari Jedkins,
JaVaughn Brown, (Middle) Tryese Whitnell, Adrian Bryant,
Terrion Barnes, (bottom) Calvion Hunter, Tranell Bridges Jr.,
Calviontae Hunter, (Right) Assistant Coach: Terry Barnes
Photo by Visual Image Photography, Inc.

The Raptors

(Back) Isaiah Lambert, Treavyon Thomas, Calvin Hunter, William
Mueller Jr., Jeremie Lackey, Angel Rodriguez (Middle) Devin Wilson,
Tyrese Hunter, (Bottom) Left: Assistant Coach: James Hunter Jr.,
Asanjai Hunter, Kamari McGee, Head Coach, Paul Hunter
Photo by Ken Lumpkin, The Insider News

The Magic

Left: Head Coach, Paul Hunter (Back) Cedric Scales,
Juan Carlos Bueno, Assistant Coach Dave George
(Middle) Trevor George, Myles Hill, Alec Pullen,
(Bottom) Ari Antreassian, Lamontae Lewis, Samad Qawi
Photo by Visual Image Photography, Inc.

One thing I say about coaching is that you develop a relationship with these guys. It's not just about basketball, but it's about building relationships and being a mentor to the next generation. That's what I enjoy being. I tell the kids all the time, "One day, you might be coaching. Try to be a mentor."

Coaching my children in basketball was fun. My son Isaiah is athletic. He is a football player also. This guy can play football. I remember the first day when he was in first grade and he played football. They had him on the line. When one of the running backs got hurt, they asked him to play running back. He got the ball for the first time and never looked back. That person lost his spot. My son is gifted and talented. He's a superstar. He's a student-athlete.

CHAPTER 11

Teenagers, Transition, and Trouble

The Challenges of Fatherhood

As with any situation in life, there are ups and downs. There will be successes, and there will certainly be failures and disappointments. There will be sunny days, and there will be difficult, cloudy days. Some of those difficult, cloudy days started to appear when my children began to make their transition from grammar school to middle school—those dreaded teenaged years. You can say that I am old-fashioned, but I believe that you need two parents in the household, and you cannot show favoritism toward your children. You cannot like one and dislike the other one. The failure I want to talk about is the mother of my children.

One big bone of contention was I did not want my children to associate with children who were disrespectful to other adults and to their own parents. If I allowed my children to do that, they would think it was all right to be disrespectful. I used to say something about not wanting Jenna to hang with this particular girl because this girl was no good, but Margarita would always contradict me which started arguments between us. Whenever we had our disagreements, I would try to be respectful because I didn't want to argue in front of my kids. I would rather we go into a room or in the car than argue in front of them.

However, she used to belittle me in front of my children. She would put me down in front of them and call me a big loser. My children saw that as they were growing up. It played a significant role in their lives because if I said no, my first daughter would run and tell her mom, "Dad said I can't go." And her mom would say, "You can go. Forget what he has to say. I did this when I was a child. My dad and mama let me do this and that." My daughter Jenna feels that she can get away with a lot of things because her mother allowed her to get away with them, but she did not let Isaiah and Victoria do the same. She was quick to tell them no, and they were quick to notice how their mother was playing favorites. She would favor Jenna over them. They saw that growing up, and today they bring that up. "You always favor Jenna. You never tell Jenna no."

So, the failure that I have made as a parent is that I should have stood up and told Margarita, "You're not going to do this." I didn't, and it cost me dearly. Not only did it cost me, but it cost my daughter. Margarita let Jenna get away with anything. Once Jenna began to make the transition, she used to come home and say, "Well, my friend's mama lets her come in at one and two o'clock in the morning. My friend's mama lets her do this." Then my kid's mother would say, "Okay, Jenna. You can go."

I would say, "Hold up. She's fifteen years old and in high school. She's not going to be coming in at twelve, one, two o'clock in the morning. I want you here at eleven-thirty." When I would say that, Margarita would contradict me. Jenna would call her on the cell phone and ask, "Mom, can I stay out until twelve-thirty?"

"Yeah, stay out until twelve-thirty."

A man cannot be effective in his home when he has the mother of his children contradicting and circumventing while she's putting him down in front of his kids. He cannot be an effective leader whatsoever. It's going to tear apart the family. It's going to divide the house against itself. There were times when my daughter used to tell me that she hated me, but I realized she hated me because I was not afraid to tell her no. She hated me because I was a father to her, and I knew that she needed structure and discipline. I was not her friend.

Her mother would not allow me to give her structure and discipline. When I used to say, "Kids, let's go for a walk or let's go ride the bikes," they would look at her and ask, "Mom, should we go with him?" She would say, "No, y'all don't have to go with him." I would say, "Come on, Victoria and Isaiah." They would do it. I was trying to get them to exercise together and enjoy ourselves together in the summer weather. When I used to tell them, "Let's clean up the house," Jenna had to go ask for her mom's approval. My little kids saw that, so as they became teenagers, they started to run to their mom. It was like they were saying, "Who is this man to tell me something?"

The fruit of all this splitting, manipulation, and getting their way soon began to manifest itself. My fifteen-year-old daughter ended up having a serious medical procedure. I was living in the house, working every day, and trying to interact with my kids. Their mom was working second shift, and she would call me and say, "Jenna is depressed. You need to talk to her."

I would say, "Depressed about what? What's a fifteen-year-old girl got to be depressed about?"

"I don't know. Go in there and talk to her," she insisted.

I would go in the room and talk to Jenna. Then I would pray with Jenna. I did not know that she had this medical procedure. Margarita knew my daughter had this operation, and she had me going in there praying with her. That's how manipulative Margarita was. She refused to tell me that my daughter had this surgery. Margarita's mother and sisters knew. I was going around them, and they never said anything. Jenna's aunt was calling her and praying for her on the phone. I never knew. I discovered that my daughter had surgery when her mother was on the computer. Jenna had her friends over, a couple of girls. They knew about it also, but they kept it hidden. It was a dirty little secret. Margarita was on the internet, and I was lying on the bed just thinking. Jenna walked in the room and asked her mother to buy her a shirt. Her mom said, "No."

Jenna said to her, "Well, forget you then since you ain't gonna buy me the shirt."

I was like, "Wait a minute. Hold up."

Margarita stood up and said to Jenna, "I do everything for you. I do more for you than I do for Victoria and Isaiah. I buy you clothes. I buy you shoes. I give you money. I even come up to your high school and take you and your friends out for lunch. I even took you to have surgery." That's when it slipped out!

I literally jumped out of the bed. I said, "What?"

My daughter ran out of the room crying because now the truth had come out. I was hurt. One thing I have learned is that you have to be mindful of what you do as a parent to your teenager. My daughter should have never had this operation. She was not mature enough to deal with the trauma associated with this type of surgical procedure. What made it bad was that Margarita and Jenna's grandmother had taken my daughter to have this operation.

I was so depressed and upset about this that I didn't know what to do. I was livid about the whole situation that my daughter at the age of fifteen had to go through all this. Margarita, the woman that I loved and who was supposed to have loved me, had kept the whole thing from me. It would have been better for her to tell me herself, even after they did it, but instead, she knew it all the time and had me going in there in the dark, counseling my daughter about her depression. That was some cold stuff.

I asked Margarita, "Why didn't you tell me what was going on? I asked you several times if Jenna was having sex. You used to tell me, 'You ask Jenna.' And like a dummy, I went in there asking, 'Jenna are you having sex with anyone?' Of course, she was going to tell me no. You had me all upset, calling me on my job, telling me that Jenna is depressed and talking about committing suicide. All the time you knew what was really going on about Jenna being depressed and wanting to commit suicide, but you refused to tell me the truth." In this case, the dirty little secret was found out. This whole circumstance was foreign to me. Though others may see having this procedure as a way to correct a mistake, I was not raised that way. That's why my mother has eighteen living children and over sixty-one grandchildren and fifty-five great-grandchildren.

I left home that night and went to my mom's homeless shelter. I did not tell my mom what had happened. I just went into her office and cried. I was just crying out because I did not want any of my children to suffer. The woman who I was supposed to have loved betrayed me by allowing my firstborn child to have this unnecessary procedure behind my back. It devastated me. I lost all respect for this woman. I wanted to get back at this woman for doing this to my child. Since I was hurting, I wanted badly to hurt her back, but I couldn't do it. I didn't want to go to jail and have my children visit me behind prison walls. To this day, I still think about it, and if I think about it too long, it still bothers me. I'm still learning to let this go. I have to move on.

Yes, I did cry many nights, asking myself what

went wrong. Anytime a parent says that they want their kids to be their best friends, they are asking for trouble. Kids already have friends. What they really need is parents, not parental buddies. If I bring you into this world, don't get it confused. I'm not your buddy, I'm your father. Parents that want to be equals with their children are headed for disaster. Kids are looking for a parent, someone who is going to give them structure and discipline, and who is going to love them and care for them. That's one of the reasons they test limits because in a strange way, they want to prove to themselves that they are loved which also means having a parent being firm enough to discipline them.

I remember receiving a call from Jenna saying that her mother put her out of the house. I asked her where she was, and she said she was at a friend's house. I said, "I want you to stay there for tonight. Then you come home in the morning. I will come and get you."

After Jenna came back home that next morning, her mother was trying to shift the blame on me. She said, "If you had only been here, if you had only done this or said that, none of this would have happened with Jenna."

I began to think, "This is crazy. Now all of a sudden I'm the reason Jenna has all these problems? Yeah, right."

Ironically, she ended up saying, "You and Jenna should get counseling." This was completely outrageous.

I remember going to see my cousin, Timmy James. He's a pastor. He told me where we could receive free counseling services. I went to this agency downtown on Sixth Street. I think it was called The Hope Place. I went there and set up a schedule to meet with the counselor, along with my daughter. We went to that first session. When we were in there, I began to cry and told the woman why I was crying.

She told my daughter, "Jenna, you see that your dad really loves you." Jenna said, "Yeah, I know." She told Jenna as she was counseling us, "Your dad is hurt because you had this operation."

Jenna said, "I know."

She said, "Jenna, he's here because he wants to see you get help because there are repercussions."

I said, "There are repercussions, Jenna, because I saw my sister and some of my friends experience this procedure. They went through some difficult things. They turned to drugs and alcohol because they were torn up on the inside. They couldn't forgive themselves nor could they relieve the pain. Their thoughts would torture them, like, 'What if I hadn't done this? How would my life be different now?'"

That counselor asked Jenna to describe how she felt about me. Jenna said, "Well, I love my dad, and I care for my dad, but my dad is a discipline guy. He's caring. He's loving. He's been there for us, and I really do love my dad. He's the best person to me. I love my dad because most of my other friends don't have their dads in their lives, and my dad has always been there for me."

The counselor said, "Jenna, describe your mother." Jenna just went on. She said, "My mom and I are best friends. My mom and I do this and that. She lets me go out. She lets me stay out. She lets me go out with older guys. She buys me things. Whatever I ask for, my mom gives to me. She never tells me no."

The counselor was sitting there analyzing what Jenna said to her. She said to Jenna, "You know you are here because your dad wants to see you get help. He doesn't want to see you go through the changes that countless others have gone through."

Jenna started to cry. Jenna and I hugged each other and cried together. Then the counselor asked Jenna to step out of the room for a minute so she could talk with me. Jenna went to sit out in the lobby. The counselor told me, "Young man, the problem is not you. As a father, it is not you. The problem is the mother of your children. She is trying to be a friend, not a parent.

You need to get her to come here because she is the one who needs help. Her mother is the one who needs to be here."

After we left the counseling, I called Margarita to let her know how it had gone. I said to her, "You need to come because she wants to have a family meeting with all of us." She didn't want it. No way. She wasn't about to touch that one and let some shrink tiptoe around in her head. She was adamant.

"Nope, I ain't going. The problem is you and Jenna, not me."

So, I left it alone. Jenna and I only went to one session, but that affirmed that this problem wasn't me. It was her mother.

I think one of the mistakes I made was letting Margarita disrespect me in front of my children. She called me names and belittled me in front of my children, her relatives, and her friends. When she got on the phone, she would talk about me like a dog, like I was nothing. I knew I was not the person she portrayed me to be. However, she is the person who has all the insecurity and esteem issues.

Looking back at it now, I can make the connection. This is how my mother had treated my father when he was in the home. The disrespect and the put-downs can drive a man to leave the home or have an affair with another woman. It can also have some very dramatic effects on the children as well.

Psychologists and behaviorists know all too well that the cycle of dysfunction tends to be multigenerational. The fact is whenever family members have to adapt to a chaotic and dysfunctional family system, that creates a new normal that has consequences for those within that sick system. The typical dysfunctional family is usually centered around one primary domineering individual who controls the family based on his or her own deep-seated insecurities. They tend to control through fear, ridicule, put-downs, physical and mental abuse.

They stifle the growth of individual family members in order to appease their sick need for control. The spinoff dysfunctions that breed in this environment are low self-esteem, feelings of inadequacy, identity crises, substance abuse, promiscuity, violence, and other risky behaviors.

In order to keep some mental balance and in order to cope, the entire family must adapt to their unbalanced family where little nurturing occurs. Adapting then becomes a dysfunctional coping mechanism that becomes thematic throughout the lives of all of the family members. This is why many of my brothers and sisters need so much help, and this is what happened to me. I became attracted to a woman who was just as domineering, manipulative, and deceptive as my mother. Those same character traits that I loathed in my mother became the basis for attraction to someone who had the same characteristics as E. Those subconscious dysfunctions were running at full speed when I entered a relationship that was doomed for destruction from the very beginning.

CHAPTER 12

It All Started to Go Wrong

In 2010 my life took an unexpected turn that cast me into the depths of depression and pain. My kids were moved far away from me to San Antonio, Texas. I was just devastated, hurt, and became deeply depressed about the whole situation. Margarita wanted me to move down there, but I decided not to go because there was just something in my spirit telling me not to go.

When Margarita broke the news to me, she had already planned it out. As usual I was the last to know. Her reasons for this move were simple: she told me that her dad was going to buy her a house and a car. I guess he had made her an offer that she couldn't refuse. Not long after I was informed, my kids moved to San Antonio.

When my kids moved to San Antonio, it was hard on them because neither Margarita nor I were there. She was still here because she had to continue to work at Chrysler until Chrysler shut down. My kids were down in San Antonio with their grandfather, Jim Muñoz.

Much of the difficulty my children were experiencing was that they didn't have any relationship with Mr. Muñoz. They didn't know anything about him because he had never been around them, and they didn't like living there.

To them it was like being uprooted to a foreign country. My kids had a very difficult time trying to adapt to the situation while waiting for their mother to join them. She tried hard to convince me to move to San Antonio. For a minute I wavered on whether or not to go, but in the end, I decided not to go. I kept experiencing an uneasiness that I just couldn't shake. It was like somebody wanted to set me up to fail. I didn't want to be drawn to a strange environment and then be set out to dry. I convinced myself that I couldn't do it. Maybe I was being a little paranoid, but I didn't feel comfortable being out of my element.

Going on past experience with Margarita, I felt I would be at a great disadvantage if I were to move with her to Texas. In Racine, when she got mad at me, she would threaten to put me out. If that happened in Texas, what in the world would I do? I didn't know anybody in Texas. The fear came in that said, "If you move down there, you know what she's going to do. She's going to put you out. She did it several times in Racine. She's going to call the police. She's going to do it in Texas." I was uneasy about the whole situation. I then made the decision not to go, but my kids moved down there with their grandfather. While Margarita was still working in Racine, she continued to call them every day, just like I did. She even communicated with them through Facebook.

However, even with all the communication among us, the kids and their grandfather kept having conflicts. One of the reasons they stayed at odds was because he used to constantly degrade me and put me down in front of the kids. My son told me that they were driving somewhere to get something to eat, and his grandfather started making derogatory statements about me, saying that I was a loser or that I was lazy. My son said that he, Victoria, and Jenna were upset. They wanted to jump on him and beat him up.

What I discovered is that no matter what issues a man has, never say anything negative about someone else's father. My kids love me unconditionally despite my shortcomings, weaknesses, or failures.

At the time my kids were living in San Antonio, Margarita and I were still living in the same house together. On one occasion, I remember she was on the phone with a friend of hers. She didn't know that I was listening in on the conversation. She must have assumed that I was gone, but I was in the basement. I heard her telling this girlfriend that her father's plan was to buy her a house, and if he did that and gave her one of his cars, she would have to leave me. I thought about it: that's the plan? Wow, I'm glad I didn't make that decision to go to Texas. Her father said to her, "I will buy you a house and give you this car if you leave Paul." In effect, Margarita traded me in for a house and a car.

When a person does something like that, they never loved you in the first place. She traded me in for material things. She never knew that I overheard that conversation, but I just played it off and went on. She was still trying to convince me to move down there. I used to say, "Yeah, I'll move down there. No, I don't want to move down there." However, I knew in my heart that I wasn't going to move down there because of her father's plan. His plan, however, didn't work.

She moved to San Antonio after Chrysler closed in October. We used to talk over the phone. I used to talk to her all the time. I also went down there and visited with my children. I stayed at the house that her father had purchased for her. I remember the first time I went down there. I was excited because I had missed my kids. I took my kids to school because that was what I used to do. They were happy to see me. I remember the first time I took the plane there. I took the bus to the airport in Milwaukee. I caught the plane to San Antonio. I rented a car and put the address in the navigation system, and it took me straight to their house. Jenna and Isaiah were there when I parked the car out front. Jenna saw me get out of the car. She told Isaiah, and they both came to the car and gave me big smiles and hugs. I asked, "Where's Victoria?" They told me where she was, and I said, "Let's go get her." We went to get her at her friend's house. She was excited to see me. She gave me a big hug and kiss. I missed my kids so much.

From there, I took them to Subway to get a sandwich. Later, their mom came. Her friends who lived in Racine were in San Antonio for Cinco de Mayo. She walked into the house with her friends. I was sitting on the couch. She looked at me and didn't say a word to me. Then she showed her friends around the house. Once she got through giving her friends a tour of the house, she told them, "My daddy bought this house for me." I was sitting there on the couch thinking, "Oh, wow. This woman did not even say "Hi, how you doing?" She did not give me a hug. This woman was supposed to be my wife, but she's not my wife. We had never gotten married, and she did not acknowledge me once she was in her home.

After she got through giving her friends a tour of the house, she came to me. "What are you doing here?" She was talking crazy. "I didn't tell you that you could come here."

I was like, "Wow!" My son and my daughter Victoria stood up to her. They said, "Every time Melissa, Letti, and your other friends are around, you are always putting Dad down. You need to stop it."

She told them, "Shut up before I slap you. You don't disrespect me." Then she told Melissa, Letti, and one of the other girls, "Come on, let's go."

Victoria came and sat beside me. She said, "Dad, every time when Melissa, Letti, and Mom's friends are around, we notice how she disrespects you."

I stayed with them while I was in San Antonio. My kids began to share information with me. They said their grandpa had told the next door neighbor that my black ass was not allowed in his house or anywhere on the premises. My kids told me this man literally hated me. I hadn't done anything to him. He would tell my kids that they didn't have a father anymore. He claimed that he was their father. He used to tell my son, "When you make it to the NFL or the NBA, don't acknowledge your father; acknowledge me. Say you learned everything from me."

My son assured me, "I told him if it wasn't for my dad, I wouldn't know how to play football or basketball."

This man is a coward. He is a prick. You cannot plant negative seeds in the heads of children, especially negative seeds about their father. I have been there for my children, whether he likes it or not. I think his problem is that I am an African-American dating his Hispanic daughter. Well, Mr. Muñoz, if in your eyes you see me as a loser, that's your problem, not mine. I am who God says I am, and that's more than a conqueror. In God's eyes, I'm a winner. In life, there will always be a Mr. Muñoz or, for that matter, a Louise Hunter. To them I say, it's not how you start off in life, it's how you finish, and I'm going to finish on top.

The next day, I got up and took my kids to school. I wanted to meet with the principal, but I couldn't meet with him. I met with the attendance officer. She was telling me that my name was not on the emergency list. I said, "Why is that?"

"They don't have you on here. You do not exist. Their father is Jim Muñoz."

I thought that was strange. I said, "That's their grandfather. I'm their father. I live in Racine, Wisconsin. I want to have access to my kids' files. I want to leave my number and contact information here in case anything happens. If you have any problems with my children, you give me a call."

She said, "I can't do that. I have to get on the phone."

She called Margarita to verify that I was actually the father. First she said, "You're not here to take the kids, are you?"

I said, "Take the kids for what?"

"Well, we were just informed that you might be sneaking down here to get your kids."

I said, "No, I just dropped my kids off. They're here."

Margarita verified that I am their father. Then they put me down as an emergency contact. I took Victoria and Isaiah to school. That's when I filled out the papers, entered my name and contact information, got access to their computer system, and the code to look at my kids' grades.

After everything was straightened out, I went back to the house and took Jenna to school. She attended East Central High School. Victoria and Isaiah were at Legacy Middle School. When I took Jenna to school, I told her I was going in to see if my name was on the emergency list. I walked into the principal's office with Jenna. I said, "This is my daughter Jenna Hunter. I'm her father. I'm here visiting my children. I want to see if you have my name down as an emergency contact."

She pulled out the card and said, "No, you don't even exist."

I said, "How can that be changed?

"The only person who can change it is Jim Muñoz."

I said to her, "He's not their father. I'm their father."

"Sir, we can't do anything about that."

I said, "Oh, okay." I told Jenna to go to her classes, and I would see her later. I told her I'd pick her up after school. When I picked her up later, I had her mother with me. I told her, "We need to get this changed in case something happens."

Her mother refused to go into the office with me to get it changed so they could contact me in case anything happened or if the teachers were having trouble with Jenna. She didn't do it. We ended up going back to the house and relaxing a little bit. Then I picked up my other two kids from school. They were very excited about that.

I want to declare that parents should not use kids as weapons to hurt one another. It's bad enough that kids have to live in a toxic environment of two separated parents because it puts them in the middle, and it scars them and affects their future relationships. It is difficult. Living my life without my kids almost made me go insane. One thing I learned from the Bible is that men will fail you. Women will fail you also.

Every day, I was just hurt by being separated from my children. The separation was as if you had cut my head in half. That's the way my heart was separated. I did not want to get up in the morning. I used to get up in the morning and tell my kids, "Jenna, it's time to get up so you can get prepared for school. Isaiah, it's time to get up. Victoria, it's time to get up." Being separated from my children destroyed me. If people knew what I was going through, they would say, "Brother, let me pray with you. If you need anything, call me. I just want to be there for you." I needed someone that had experienced that in their life to assist me. No man, no woman, should be separated from their children. It almost killed me.

I was so depressed that there were times that I just didn't want to do anything. I didn't want to interact with anyone. "What am I going to do? I'm depressed. I'm hurt. What can I do?" No one knew how close to the edge I was. No one knew how desperately fragile I was. When I woke up in the morning, I didn't want to get out of bed. I didn't want to work out or go to the gym and do a couple of sets and then hit the whirlpool and the sauna. To add insult to injury, I had to move back to Love and Charity Homeless Shelter and be around my mother and all her issues. It just seemed like there was no way out of this bottomless pit of depression.

I lost everything. I lost the home. I lost the cars. I was depressed about living at Love and Charity. I was devastated. I wish someone had been there to share their experience with me, but no one was there to assist me. I had to go through this adversity by myself, but it made me a better person and a better man. When you go through adversity, there is a blessing at the end. Remember that.

I remember talking to a friend at Love and Charity named Michael. He was a former attorney who was living there at the time. I remember him telling me, "She cannot take your child out of state. If it's over one-hundred-fifty miles, she has to get court permission to take your child out of state."

Armed with what I thought was good legal advice, I went down to complain to child support. I wanted to find out who the case manager was. When I went down there, they were vague and didn't want to give me any information. I got frustrated and ended up leaving. I missed my kids, and I wanted them back here with me. A couple of months later, I went back to child support and told one of the clerks, "I need to find out who the case manager is." The young girl told me the case manager's name was Mrs. Fields. I then asked the clerk if Mrs. Fields was black or white. The clerk said she's African-American. I said, "Okay, give me her number because I want to set up an appointment to meet with her." She gave me the number. I called Mrs. Fields and did not get a response. I decided to go back down to child support, and I told the young lady, "You gave me her number. I called and left a message. I would like to see her."

She said, "Well, she's not in today."

I said, "Okay." I ended up leaving. Before I left, I

began to tell that young lady that it's not right. She asked what is not right. I said, "My children are living in another state, and the mother of my children did not take me to court to get permission from a judge to move my kids out of the state." I asked where the parenting book was that said that a parent could not move the kids out of the state.

She said, "The books are over there."

I went to the books and said, "I'm going to take this home, and I will be back." I took the book home and read that in order for a parent to take the kids out of the state over one-hundred-fifty miles, they must petition the court. She did not do that. She just did what she wanted to do in order to get a house and a car from her dad.

The next day, I met with the case manager, Mrs. Fields. This woman was rude to me. When I told her the situation, she told me, "Oh, she did?"

I said, "She ended up sending these certified letters in the mail telling me that she is leaving the state."

The case manager looked at the letter and said, "Well, those are her kids. She can do what she wants to do. There is nothing I can do to assist you."

I was hurt. I said, "You can assist me because it says in this book that she was supposed to have taken me to court."

"Well, she sent you a certified letter, so that's good enough."

I was just shocked. I told her, "You mean to tell me, if I get on the plane and go down there and snatch my kids out of school and bring them back here, there's not going to be an Amber Alert out on me in San Antonio that I kidnapped my kids?"

"Well, you know what, young man? You do what you got to do, but there's nothing we can do about it. Those are her kids. She can do what she wants to with her kids. We don't get involved in that. I'm just a case manager. We don't get involved in any of that stuff. You have to take her to court. That's your job. She sent you a letter. That's good enough. She doesn't have to petition the court, you do. She sent you a certified letter letting you know that she was taking the kids out of state. That's good enough. There's nothing we can do."

I left there angry and upset. I really wanted to slap this woman. I lost faith in the child support system. When you can take a man's child or a woman's child out of the state without petitioning the court and child support cannot assist, there is something wrong with the system. The system has to get better. I believe if the system of Racine child support could have a makeover, it would be great. They could review people every six months, making sure that the father is getting visitation rights, the mother is getting visitation rights, and everything is balanced out. The case manager was no help to me.

What I discovered was that the case manager had been giving Margarita advice. That's why she sent me certified letters because Mrs. Fields had informed her to do that. It was totally wrong for her to do that. The way I found out is that Margarita ended up telling me herself. A case manager is not supposed to give legal advice. It is not their job. Their job is to manage the case. I was upset. It was like wherever I turned my head, I couldn't get any help.

For some reason, this case manager was against me. I kind of gave up. Then I ended up receiving a letter in the mail to attend court because I was asking for a reduction in child support. I went to court with Margarita for a petition. That's when I was informed that Mrs. Fields was no longer with the child support agency, and we were going to be assigned a new caseworker. It took a while to get assigned, but Margarita was living out of state. When I did get a chance to meet with the new caseworker, he told me that Mrs. Fields should not have been giving Ms. Muñoz legal advice. I told him, "I miss my kids every day. I pay child support, and this woman complains about me and my child support that she's receiving every week. She took my kids out of state, and she wants me to send extra money. I'm not sending her any extra money because she should not have taken my kids out of the state."

I was hurt that she did it, but I had to move on. I was able to do that. I look back on Mrs. Fields, the case manager and say, "What's in it for you? What have I done to you? You should have told Margarita, 'No, you cannot take the kids out of state unless you petition the court. That is a violation.'" That's what Mrs. Fields should have told the mother of my children, but she gave her legal advice. That's why I contend that the child support system is broken. It needs to be fixed immediately.

I've promised myself that once I get the money, I am going after my children. I am going to fight their mother with every cent that I have. I am going to fight because it's a father's right to have a relationship with his kids. Parents deserve to have a relationship with their children, and no one is going to stop me. And I mean no one.

I don't hate the caseworker. I don't despise her. The only thing I can say is she should do her job. Be a case manager, not a lawyer.

CHAPTER 13

The Road to Success, the College Years

With all that had been going on in my life, I had refused to let the difficulties stop me from reaching my goal of graduating from college. After coming up in a highly dysfunctional family, where all our dysfunctions became the norm that too often dictated our destiny, I was determined not to be derailed by distractions but to stay focused on becoming a success despite all the overwhelming odds. I had no father in the home. My mother was dead set against even the idea of being educated. She loathed educated people. I had several brothers and sisters who had become victims of drug and alcohol addiction, who had never gone further than high school and suffered long bouts of unemployment. Nevertheless I was determined. Despite having my own emotional depression, a failed relationship with Margarita, and separation from my children, it seemed that my only way out was to finish college with a degree in Business Administration.

For a long time now, I have wanted to be a successful executive who owned his own business, but I knew I needed credentials and that a good education would be the gateway to my success. Success can be defined in many ways. However, it's not just money and obtaining material wealth. No, for me success means much more. Success means achieving my goals to rise above the emotional restrictions that had been imposed upon me by my own mother. My mother wanted to see her kids, especially me, fail. My mother built an empire to help others while neglecting and withholding love and emotional support from the twenty-one children that she brought into this world.

This is why I am going to make it. Not only do I want to prove to my mother that I am a success, but I want to be an example to my own sons and daughters and brothers and sisters. Hope and dreams are obtainable things if you trust in God and let go of the past. Despite everything you have experienced or have been told, you can make it if you try.

I graduated from Washington Park High School in 1990. It was a happy moment in my life. I'll never forget walking across the stage and being handed my diploma while shaking hands with the principal. On this occasion, my mother and some of my brothers and sisters were there cheering me on. That experience really did something positive for my spirit. It gave me a taste of what it was like to accomplish something academically, and I wanted more. I didn't just want to stop with high school, I wanted to go all the way. However, I had plans to take a year off and then go to college.

Jackson State University, Mississippi

The first college that I attended after taking a year off was Jackson State University in Jackson, Mississippi. Unfortunately, I was only there for about one semester because I got sick and discovered that I had

Bell's Palsy which is a condition that affects the facial nerve and paralyzes one side of your face. In my case, I couldn't feel anything on the left side of my face. At night, I had to tape my eye shut. If I didn't, I could have gone blind. I came back home to Racine. I was on medication for a while. My physician told me that this can stay with you for years, or it can go away in a few months. This issue had me very concerned because I didn't want to go through this for years, every day taping my eye down when I went to bed and having to massage the side of my face three times a day. By the grace of God, within a month the Bell's Palsy disappeared. I was happy about that.

Northern State University, South Dakota

With that short setback behind me, I decided to attend Northern State University in South Dakota. I remember taking the bus there, meeting people along the way, and having conversations with them. I had a great time there. It was during the winter when I got there. It was cold. There was a snow storm the day I arrived. I got situated and started to sign up for my classes. I started to meet people on campus. A lot of classes I had to take were remedial because I had to bring up my GPA and academic skills in order to stay enrolled. I really liked it there, but I never really found my niche. I was like a lost individual. I didn't know where to go to get assistance in academics. I didn't know how to use the resources that were available. Therefore, sadly, I ended up dropping out. I came back to Racine and tried Gateway Technical College.

Gateway Technical College

I didn't like Gateway at all because I felt lost there too, but I remember taking a pre-tech writing course taught by Valerie Hennen. After failing that course the first time around, I almost gave up and threw in the towel. At that moment, I declared that college wasn't for me, and I wasn't coming back next semester. I remember telling Mrs. Hennen that I was going to drop out. She said, "No, don't drop out. Just continue." A few days later, I watched a television documentary on Frederick Douglass. In one of his many famous quotes, he said that without struggle, there is no progress. To use a contemporary idiom, *"No pain, no gain."* At that defining moment in my life, those words resonated within my spirit. They revived my desire and will to overcome adversity and gave me the courage to face my fear of failure.

Paul Hunter and Valerie Hennen Photo by Paul Hunter

Inspired by Frederick Douglass' immortal words, I found new resolve. I declared that I was going back to Gateway Technical College because, after all, I was still making progress even though I had failed that class. There are many battles that are lost on the way to winning a war. The war was the bigger picture. I learned to focus on the bigger picture and not get bogged down in depression simply because I'd lost a single battle. I learned from my mistakes and pressed on towards my goal.

Therefore, I went back the following semester and took that course again, this time passing it with a D. Passing wasn't good enough for me. Deep within my heart, I knew I could do better, so I decided to take that class a third time, and I passed it with a B. That's when I discovered that I had what it takes to be successful in college—determination and an undying will to succeed. Even though there were plenty of times that I wanted to take the easy route and drop out of school, I refused to let the enemy (the enemy within me) prevail.

Another factor that contributed to my success at Gateway was that Mrs. Hennen advised me about all the resources that were available there to help students succeed. I was unaware of all of the assistance available to struggling students. For example, if you have a learning disability, they have support available for students with those special needs. I believe that the main factors in students falling behind in college are that they are not adequately prepared for college in the first place, and second, support and assistance available to keep you in school are underutilized.

The Academic Support Center (ASC) is another resource that students can use at Gateway. I spent many hours there, receiving the tutoring and academic skills-building support that I needed. When you come into that facility, you are greeted by Diane Ingalsbe or Dawn Kelley, or some of the other staff. The ASC is a completely helpful place. You can pass your courses if you don't give up, swallow your pride, and ask for help. I suggest that every student who needs it should come to the ASC because they are going to get the best academic support that is available at Gateway. I practically lived there.

Diane Ingalsbe, Paul Hunter, and Dawn Kelley
Photo by Paul Hunter

That's how I passed my courses. If it wasn't for the ASC, I believe I would not have received my first degree, an associate's degree in supervisory management.

Another resource at Gateway is the Multicultural Center which is run by Janet Days. It is helpful for students to learn to interact with students of other cultures. There you learn to be culturally sensitive and think beyond the perimeter of your own cultural mores. Being exposed to a multicultural environment better prepares you for a global economy and marketplace.

I also utilized the Gateway library. It has been upgraded. You have access to the internet, to books, to the staff. The staff—April Gandy, Rachel Rohlf, and Lauren Robb—is very helpful. These people are there to assist

Paul Hunter, Rachel Rohlf, April Gandy, and Lauren Robb
Photo by Paul Hunter

students. Take advantage of all of the library resources available.

Graduating from Gateway

I graduated in 2005 from Gateway Technical. I was the first child of my mother's twenty-one natural children to receive an associate's degree in supervisory management. The day that I graduated from college, I

Connie Hunter, Paul Hunter, and Keysha Perry
Photo provided by Paul Hunter

was clearly excited. My sister Connie came. My niece Keysha Perry came.My mother was supposed to have come, but she did not come to my graduation. I was hurt. I was devastated that she did not come. After graduation, I took pictures with my niece and my sister. I took pictures with a friend and mentor, Michael Mulhern.

Paul Hunter and Michael Mulhern Photo by Paul Hunter

My mother had an invitation to come to my graduation, but she refused to come. I took the initiative after graduation to go to where she was, and that was the Love and Charity Homeless Shelter. I drove there, so I could show her my degree. When I walked in, Chris (a resident at that time) was happy to see me. Some of the other residents were too. I had on my cap and gown. I asked Chris, "Why didn't you bring my mother to my ceremony?"

He said to me, "Paul, I really don't want to tell you."

I said, "Chris, please tell me because I need to know."

Chris told me, "Paul, your mother said, 'I'm not going to his graduation. He's not important to me. He'll never be important to me because I got Love and Charity. I might not have no education, but I got Love and Charity, and I'm the director. I got three cars sitting outside. So what, he got his associate's degree? He'll never be more important to me. Look what I got!'"

I asked, "Did she really say that, Chris?"

Chris said, "Yes."

Then the other residents agreed with Chris that she had said that. I continued to smile, but I was hurting on the inside. I said, "Chris, can you run upstairs and tell my mother that I am here, and I would like to take a picture with her?" Chris went upstairs to get my mom. I had my camera. My mother would not even give me a hug or say, "Son, I'm happy for you. Job well done! I'm proud that you accomplished this. This is a great day." When we were standing in the kitchen with my mom, I said, "Chris, here's the camera. E, come on and take a picture with me." However, she refused to take a picture with me and used multiple excuses. I said, "It's just a picture. That's all it is, just a picture with me wearing my cap and gown and holding my certificate."

She said, "I can't do it. Look at my hair. I don't have on the right shoes. I don't have on the right dress.

I don't have on the right clothes." It was excuse after excuse. Those were the signs of jealousy of her own son. Since she didn't want to take a picture, she just turned and walked away. She said, "I'm going back upstairs." I asked the residents of Love and Charity if they wanted to take a picture with me. They agreed. They obliged. I took pictures with former residents and homeless people that day

I didn't take any pictures with my mom. I was hurt. I was just baffled by the whole situation. It was a day of celebration, but she was not pleased with me. Before I left, I went upstairs to see my mama. I said to her, "I'm getting ready to go home. My kids and I are going out to eat."

My mother said to me, "Son, a child is not supposed to be successful in life until the parents are deceased."

Oh my God, that statement blew me away. Talk about being crushed. It was like being broadsided by an eighteen-wheel truck. I never saw it coming. It was very lonely walking downstairs from my mother's apartment at the mission. I was dizzy, confused about what this woman had just said to me. What she said stayed in my mind for a very long time. I couldn't understand it. I probably will never understand it.

You see, as messed up as my mother is, as singled-minded and coldhearted as my mother is, as emotionally detached and neglectful as my mother is—she's still my mother. I love her. I have always loved her. My brothers and sisters, many of whom are messed up to this very day because of how my mother's heartless treatment left them emotionally bruised and damaged, love her too. All I wanted was to be appreciated, to be validated, to share a great milestone in my life as the first out of twenty-one children to graduate from college. All I wanted was for her to be there on this monumental day of my life, but she refused to come. I was willing to overlook her not being there for me.

I came to the mission where she was, but she refused to even take a picture with me, to capture this celebratory moment in time. It was an appropriate opportunity to simply be happy for me for once in my life, yet she was so stubborn and heartless that she manifested herself as a hater, and had the unmitigated gall to utter the coldest words imaginable to me.

I walked down the steps, left the mission, got into my car, and went home to my kids and Margarita. Ironically, they couldn't get to the ceremony either because they had gotten lost on the way. I took pictures with my kids at the house, and we all celebrated as a family. I didn't let my mother's ineptness squelch my resolve to achieve.It only solidified my determination to be a success.

Jenna Hunter, Victoria Hunter, and Isaiah Hunter Munoz
Photo provided by Paul Hunter

Upper Iowa University

In 2010 I enrolled in Upper Iowa University. I remember the first time I made the decision to go back to school to obtain a bachelor's degree so I could get a better job, do things I wanted to do, and earn the income that I wanted. I remember walking into that office and being met by Lynne Zygowski. Lynne is very passionate about assisting students. She put together a career plan for me. She told me the classes that I needed to take in order to graduate. She was very helpful, kind, and honest. Handing me the career plan she had already devel-

Lynne Zygowski and Paul Hunter Photo provided by Paul Hunter

oped, she gave me these encouraging words, "Mr. Hunter, you can succeed here at Upper Iowa University."

Upper Iowa University is a great university. It has resources that students should use. One of the things I like about Upper Iowa University is its professors. Never in my pursuit of higher education have I experienced the passion that these professors exhibit in wanting to see their students succeed. They want to see their students' weaknesses turn into strengths. They want to see their students walk out of there confident and bold, not arrogant, but confident.

In my opinion, it is one of the best universities in the country. You have the Milwaukee campus, the Racine campus, the Elkhorn campus, and the headquarters in Fayette, Iowa. It's a great university. It is unique because they don't go by semesters, they go by terms. You attend for eight weeks, and then you start a new course. It's accelerated. Term one, I ended up taking an English course and a biology course. I was on the

Dean's List for the first time. Never in my life had I ever been on the Dean's List. When I was sharing this information with some fellow students, they became jealous. It goes to show that not everyone is happy for your success.

Even Margarita sent me a negative text in response to the text that I sent her informing her that I had made the Dean's List. Surprisingly, I even received a negative response from my daughter Jenna. However, I believe that it was really Margarita who responded. One thing I have learned in life is that you are going to have some haters. When you have haters, say hi and bye, and just keep on walking and let them say what they will.

Upper Iowa University was a struggle at times. I kept in mind what Frederick Douglass said: without struggle, there is no progress. In anything that we do, we will struggle, but we will make progress. Upper Iowa University has been great to me. I'm going to miss the school because of the relationships that I have had with the professors, students, and staff.

Students attending universities or any technical colleges meet with their academic advisors and counselors. Every year at Upper Iowa University I received an email regarding scholarships, writing essays to get extra money! Students should take advantage of that and use every resource available. I'm just an ordinary guy who came from the hood. I learned how to speak and write well. I came from the hood to a technical college to earn an associate's degree in supervisory management and have now graduated from Upper Iowa University, earning a bachelor's degree in business administration. God has been good to me. He has put me around positive people.

Academic Struggles

Some of my struggles have been academic. Some of the academics were unfamiliar to me. Sometimes I had to sit there and read chapter after chapter, but it brought discipline into my life. I had to set aside time to study and do homework. I believe everybody struggles in some area of academics. I struggled, but I managed to make progress. I'm going to continue to struggle, but I will make progress. I will improve. I will continue to work hard. I will continue to educate myself. I will continue to learn. Learning sometimes can be very difficult, but I will keep at it.

Had it not been for some key people who were involved in my life, I would not have graduated with my bachelor's degree. If it wasn't for getting daily devotions from Joel and Victoria Osteen, I would not have made it. Here is one of the daily devotions that really helped me out. It says, "Calling forth seeds of greatness." It came from Jeremiah 17:7, that says: "Blessed is one who trusts in the Lord, whose confidence is in him."

If it wasn't for these daily devotions that were coming to me Monday through Friday, I would not have made it. I'm being honest. Another daily devotion that came from Joel and Victoria Osteen was "The Reward is Set in Place." What I got from that is that my degree has been set in place. That came from Jeremiah 29:13: "You will seek me and find me when ye seek me with all your heart."

Those daily devotions were very encourging, and they inspired me because I was so burdened from growing up in a dysfunctional family. My mind needed renewing, and my spirit needed to be revived. Thank God that I found both through this wonderful inspirational literature.

CHAPTER 14
The Graduate

Saturday, May 5th, 2012, was one of the greatest days in my life because on that day I graduated from Upper Iowa University with my bachelor's degree in Business Administration. As any graduate can tell you, graduating from college is the culmination of academic achievement. It demands great struggle and sacrifice. There had been all of the long hours of burning the midnight oil, studying literally thousands of pages of academic literature in various complex subjects, grueling examinations, and countless hours in the classroom, not to mention writing hundreds of pages for research papers—all of it necessary, but none of it easy.

Graduating from college in my forties was a formidable task in and of itself, but my age also made it more gratifying. In many of my classes I was the oldest person in the class, but I wasn't the oldest in my graduating class of 2012. Thank God. That distinction went to someone else. However, the most important distinction that I proudly wear is that I am the first in the Hunter family to graduate from college with a four-year degree. More than anything else, I relish the fact that I am the first in three generations of Hunters to reach the summit of that baccalaureate mountain.

As I was getting prepared for graduation, I was very excited. I was like a restless child the night before Christmas, anticipating the joy tomorrow would bring. There was, however, this one major difference: my degree was not a gift. It was something I had earned.

On this momentous occasion I wasn't just happy for myself, I was happy for all of my family. In my mind I imagined myself walking across that stage, and with me would be my mother, my siblings, my nephews, nieces and cousins; looking down from heaven would be my father and Thomas. In a real sense, if I graduated, they all graduated because my success would open the door of possibility for all the generations of Hunters. While I do not wish to trivialize my graduating with a cliché like, "If I can do it, you can do it," however, that saying really does reflect my desire to see my kinfolk succeed in life too.

The Lonely Ride to Iowa

To demonstrate how close this issue is to my heart, a year prior to my graduation, I indicated to my siblings that they should start preparing to come to my graduation. I so badly wanted them to be there, to share the moment with me. I wanted them to see a successful sibling graduating from college so they in turn could internalize this as their own experience. I wanted them to be able to reach beyond their current reality into the realm of greater possibility. Unfortunately, it didn't happen that way, and all my desire to share with them melted away into a puddle of wishful thinking and disappointment.

My out-of-town siblings could not attend my graduation ceremony. That was disappointing but understandable. However, most of my siblings and relatives who live in Racine, Wisconsin, indicated that they were going to come. After hearing that, I was full of joy. It made me very happy to know that my siblings, who had all been through so much together, would share this auspicious occasion with me.

As graduation day drew closer, I decided to rent a fifteen-passenger van so that we could all drive together to Iowa. Even then, I was imagining the fun we would have as we all rode up there together, reminiscing, laughing and joking, just being a happy sibling group en route to support their youngest brother. I also took care of all the hotel accommodations by charging the expenses to my credit card. Once again, I checked with each one of them, and they all said, "We're coming, Paul. We will be there."

From my history with my siblings and relatives, I knew there was a chance that I was stepping out on a limb by funding their trip to Iowa. Of course, those of my siblings who were working faced the possibility of not being able to get the time off. Although I could understand that situation, my brothers and sisters who weren't working had no excuse not to come. Then I found out that my brothers and sisters who had promised to come would not show up for my graduation.

I was devastated. All that time, they had led me on, only to pull out at the last minute. Fortunately, I was able to cancel the hotel and maxi-van reservations in time before I lost the money. When it came time for me to leave, I went to Enterprise and rented a compact car for myself, and at approximately 3:00 a.m., I began the six-hour drive to Iowa, alone.

My mother wasn't going to go either. Honestly, there were two reasons why I didn't want her to come. The first reason was how she had treated me when I graduated from Gateway Technical College. E had two tickets to the graduation ceremony, and she didn't care enough about me to show up. The second reason was because leading up to my graduation, she was saying that I wasn't going to graduate. Several times, out of her own mouth, she made derogatory statements in reference to my graduation, even going as far as saying to my siblings, "That negro ain't gonna graduate." Once again, my feelings were trampled upon, but I didn't let it stop me. As a matter of fact, I like to think of it this way: I graduated from college *despite* what E said.

Graduation Eve

During the long drive to Iowa, it was mile after mile of cornfields and farmland just as you typically see driving through Wisconsin—a drive that I have taken on any number of occasions. While driving, I refused to spend time thinking about how E and my siblings weren't going to be there. No, I didn't allow their lack of consideration and their insensitivity to encroach upon this joyous graduation journey. The closer I got to Iowa, the happier I became.

When I finally arrived on campus, I looked around at all the beautiful surroundings, the campus grounds and the buildings, and I was enthralled. It was almost like entering the Emerald City in the land of Oz. There was an air of excitement, and the campus seemed to be all aglow. Now that I was in the graduating class of 2012, my perspective of the college had changed. This once-forbidding institution of higher learning where I had struggled so had now become an endearing place that for the rest of my life I would proudly call my alma mater. Graciously, Upper Iowa University welcomed me home.

After strolling through the campus grounds and taking in all of the beautiful sights, I decided it was time to go pick up my cap and gown. Before I knew it, time had gotten away from me. It was late morning, and I had to leave campus to go check in at the Best Western Hotel in Independence, Iowa, a fifty-minute drive from Fayette, where the campus was located.

The Interview

The Best Western Hotel was very nice, and the hotel staff were equally nice and accommodating. With not much time to spare, I hurried to my room to change clothes because I had an interview scheduled back in Fayette with Janell Bradley, contributing writer for the Fayette Leader, the local newspaper. Like most people who have heard my story, Janell was fascinated to hear about all of the vicissitudes that I have experienced in life. The odds were, I wasn't supposed to make it—but here I was, not only telling my story, but graduating from college.

During the interview I was able to give Janell a candid and brutally honest overview of life being raised in a highly dysfunctional family. I talked about all of the trials and tribulations, and I recounted how dysfunction, depression, and despondency were the only familial legacies my mother had passed down to her large brood of children. On one hand, it was easy to talk about all of the negatives of my past; doing so actually turned out to be cathartic. On the other hand, while engaged in the interview, I was hurting. I was torn inside. No, I didn't let on to that during the interview because just as in times past, I was smiling on the outside but crying and broken down on the inside. Yes, I was good at giving the story, saying all the right things. All of my brothers and sisters learned that skill from being around the Love and Charity Mission. That's the one thing E taught us all to do well: smile for the camera, tell the story, just don't tell the whole truth.

I was hurting during that interview because I had to deal with the contradiction that I was from a family that was famous for being so large, but not a one of them was there for support or to be a source of encouragement to me. I got through the interview by staying focused because if I would have drifted too far into the stark reality of the painful truth, I would not have been able to keep my composure.

So, why didn't anyone show up? I'm not sure whether E influenced my brothers and sisters and persuaded them not to come or whether jealousy and envy caused them to not want to come on their own. Whatever the case, I was surrounded by thousands of loved ones from my fellow graduates' families, but not one Hunter showed up for me.

After the interview, Janell and I went outside so she could take photographs of me to go along with the article. By this time Janell had been impacted by my story. She was really taken aback by all of the unbelievable hardships and obstacles that I had to endure and overcome in order to graduate. After she took the pictures, Janell walked up to me and said that since no one from my family would be there to cheer for me when I walked across the stage, she was going to be there to scream out my name and cheer for me when they called me to the stage and handed me my degree. Wow, when Janell said those heartwarming words, my eyes welled up with tears of joy. Thank God, somebody cared.

After the interview was over, I returned to my hotel room for a time of introspection, and I did an assessment of myself. During that time of reflection and forethought, I determined that from here on out, the people that I would associate with should be people who are positive and doing something constructive with their lives. One thing that I have learned over the years is that dysfunctional people are drawn to other dysfunctional people. That's how dysfunctions perpetuate down through multiple generations, just like they have in my family. I made a promise to myself and to God that the dysfunction would stop right here. I have made a covenant with my own heart to go forward and never turn back.

❖❖❖❖❖❖❖

Graduation Day

The next morning was graduation day. I got up and prepared for a long, exciting day. I never will forget how when I was in the hotel lobby, I saw many families beaming with pride over their sons and daughters who were graduating. They were there to support their children. On one hand, it was beautiful to see, and I was glad for them, but on the other hand, it tore me up on the inside to know that there would be not one person from my family there to cheer for and support me. There was no one there from my family to encourage me. However, it was at that very moment that I remembered what the Bible said David did when no one encouraged him during a very trying time—he encouraged himself, and that's exactly what I did. I encouraged myself. I jumped into my car and headed from Independence, Iowa, to the campus of Upper Iowa University, where in just a few hours I would become a graduate.

One of the first things that I had to do when I arrived on campus was a photo shoot. It was great; I loved it because it was a great, celebratory moment. Finally, I was not in the shadow of E as secondary subject matter in one of her media events. No, not this time. It was all about me and my accomplishments and how I made it, even without the support of my family.

After the photo shoot, it was time for all the graduates to line up. There were many colleges at the university that were graduating students, so we all had to line up according to our disciplines. Additionally, Upper Iowa has extension sites throughout Iowa and Wisconsin. There were students from the Milwaukee, Elkhorn, Des Moines, and Fayette centers, and that's how we had to line up, according to our disciplines and locations. There we all were, hundreds of us, all anxiously waiting our turn to walk across the stage to receive our coveted degrees.

Soon the procession into the gymnasium began.

The anticipation and excitement were palpable. All of us were ecstatic that we had made it. Most were happy that their families were there to share the momentous occasion with them. As for me, I kept my mind focused on the purpose for which I had come to this great institution of higher learning—to finish my studies. In that moment I realized I didn't have time to be concerned about who wasn't there because the most important thing was that I was about to graduate with my degree in Business Administration.

We proudly marched into the gymnasium with "Pomp and Circumstance" blaring over the P.A. system. The gymnasium was filled to capacity. Immediately, some of the students became a little nervous because it was so overwhelming. I remember telling my group the same thing I used to say to the kids on my basketball team during the championship game years ago: "Don't let it bother you. Just act like you've been here before." Confidently we took our seats and sat through the commencement speech. Now the time came for us to receive our degrees.

They Cheered Me On

A young lady in our graduating class named Dominica Stewart asked me, "Mr. Paul, is there no one here to cheer for you when you receive your degree?" "No, no one is here to cheer me on," I replied. She responded by saying, "That's all right, I will cheer you on."

And then another young lady named Jasmine Lohr said, "I will too." When it came time for me to receive my degree, out of the thousands that were there I could hear two of them, Dominique and Jasmine, cheering me on. I thank God for those two angels who took the time to care about me.

❖❖❖❖❖❖❖

Paul Hunter and Dominica Stewart
Photo provided by Paul Hunter

Jasmine Lohr and Paul Hunter
Photo provided by Paul Hunter

I was enthusiastic to be called to the stage to receive my diploma. I was excited to walk across the brilliant stage amongst the esteemed faculty members, with the spotlight of achievement beaming down upon me. I was excited to shake the dean's hand and to hear him say, "Congratulations, Mr. Hunter." And in the background I could hear those three ladies cheering me on. Despite my loneliness and my broken heart, they cheered me on. Despite all of the family's dysfunctions, it made no difference, and they cheered me on. Despite the discouragement and the two faces of E that I have had to endure year after year, those ladies cheered me on. Despite the fact that my siblings refused to come, they cheered me on. Yes indeed, God raised up other witnesses to be there at the finish line to cheer me on. It was a long race, an academic triathlon, but I didn't quit. I stayed in the race, and I finished my degree. One thing I can say, though, had it not been for the Lord being on my side, I never would have made it.

After we all received our degrees, we happily returned to our seats. There was one thing left for us to do, one simple yet culminating act that remained. From the stage, the dean of students gave these instructions, "Graduating class of 2012, move your tassels from the right side to the left." And in unison with the simple move of our tassels from right to left, we were now officially the graduating class of 2012. With that announcement, the entire gymnasium was ecstatic. We hugged, we high-fived each other, we shook hands. Together all of us shared this magical moment of victory and celebration.

I was excited for what I had achieved in my life. By being the first one to graduate from college, I have laid a foundation for the Hunter family to build upon. Since Paul, a neglected, fatherless, and, at times, angry and confused child had done it. I know others in my family could do it too.

As we marched out of the gymnasium, I was filled with happiness and joy and a great sense of accomplishment. For a moment I had forgotten my pain, that I had stood there alone. As the old saying goes, "Blood is thicker than water." There is nothing like having the support of your family. All I had ever known was family, but to stand there without the presence of any of them was almost unfathomable.

I watched family after family congratulating their children, some hugging, kissing, even crying. I saw families that had three generations there in support of their graduates. There were grandparents, parents and siblings all taking photographs together, presenting flowers, cards, and other gifts. It was a happy moment for everyone. This was hard for me to watch, but I realized that I couldn't help but to be happy for those whose families thought enough about them to be there to share the moment.

However, I remembered that I had to encourage myself. It was through this experience that I learned to turn my pain into power. You see, the more you hurt me, the more determined I become to achieve, to be better, to be greater, to excel to the highest heights. When you hurt me, you make me want to fight, not a physical fight, but a battle of the will, to use mind over matter. I become, as the Bible says, more than a conqueror. It was at that moment that I understood that the purpose that God has for me is bigger than what my mother, my siblings, and everyone else has ever understood. It's bigger than what people feel about me.

Therefore, despite my past, despite my upbringing, despite my disadvantages, despite my poverty, despite my labeling, and despite my shortcomings, I am and shall always be a college graduate. I am a person who is on the move. I am a person who can do all things, through Christ who strengthens me.

Through adversity, through trials and tribulations, this man has made it. This man has accomplished something that his family members tried to prevent. They put obstacles in his way and tried their best to discourage him and pull him down, but this man made it anyhow.

As I end this book, I want all to know that I hold no animosity against my family members because not even they could stop me from being successful. When I graduated, history was made in the Hunter family. I pray that there will be others who make it too until we can all rise to the prominence and status that God has planned for such a great family.

The Bible says in Ephesians 6:2, "To honor thy father and mother." However, some would say that I have not kept this commandment by revealing sensitive information about my mother. To that criticism I would sincerely respond that I have honored my mother by doing on her behalf what she has not been able to do on her own—face the truth. The Bible also says, "The truth shall make you free." By shedding light on my family's issues, there are fewer places for dysfunction to hide. Perhaps now all of us can find the road to freedom, wholeness, and prosperity. As for me, I have found that road and have begun a new leg of my life's journey. I have plans to put my degree to work and start a business of my own.

I want to give sincere thanks to all of you who have helped me along the way because I could not have made it alone. Despite all of the circumstances that came to destroy me and steal my destiny, I can truly say that I am Paul Lamar Hunter, the 19th child, and now and forever, a story of success.

Paul Hunter receives his degree from
Dr. David Chown,
Chief Academic Officer of Upper Iowa University,
Graduating Class of 2012

THE END

UPPER IOWA UNIVERSITY
Established in 1857®

I am pleased to have been able to share some information about my alma mater, Upper Iowa University, in this book. I could not have accomplished my degree in the manner I did without the support of UIU faculty and staff, whom I appreciate very much. If readers are interested in finding out more about Upper Iowa University, I recommend the website www.uiu.edu.

Life To Legacy

Let us bring your story to life! With Life to Legacy, we offer the following publishing services: Manuscript development, editing and transcription services, ghostwriting, cover design, copyright services, ISBN assignment, worldwide distribution and eBooks. You maintain control over your project because we are here to serve you.

Even if you do not have a manuscript, we can ghostwrite your story for you from audio recordings and even legible handwritten documents.

We also specialize in family history books, so you can leave a written legacy for your children, grandchildren and others. You put your story in our hands, and we'll bring it to literary life!

Please visit our website:
www.Life2legacy.com, or call us at 877-267-7477
You can also email us at: Life2legacybooks@att.net